CONTENTS

Author's Preface

This small book is not intended to be a history of the Freemen of Newcastle upon Tyne; it is more a series of essays upon various aspects of that history, with the object of showing their development over the centuries. One of the major difficulties in preparing any account of the Freemen as an organisation over the long period since their appearance in the twelfth century (leaving aside any unrecorded existence before then) is the scattered nature of the available information. The seeker in this field is in great difficulty if he does not know where to look for information and, when found, correlating individual items into a connected whole. It is my hope that these essays may make that task a little easier by at least giving some indication where information may be found. They may also indicate a few cases where statements of former authors seem to be erroneous in the light of information now available which was not previously known or was overlooked or misinterpreted.

I have intentionally omitted much from the essays, because to have reproduced all available information would render them very tedious. Attention has therefore been concentrated more on matters forgotten or generally unknown. This may lead readers to consider the essays superficial but perhaps they may find what has been included stimulates enquiring minds into further research: this is a vast field and there is room for more research, if only to demonstrate that some of my conclusions are not adequately supported or even incorrect. If any readers should take time to study these matters they will find the task most interesting - the byeways of history can be much more exciting than the main roads.

THE FREEMEN OF
NEWCASTLE UPON TYNE

THE INSTITUTIONS AND HISTORY

of

THE FREEMEN OF

NEWCASTLE UPON TYNE

by

R. F. WALKER, M.A., LL.M.

Published by
The Stewards' Committee of
The Freemen of Newcastle upon Tyne

ISBN 0 9527338 0 3

Produced by J. & P. Bealls Ltd., Gallowgate, Newcastle.

REFERENCE ABBREVIATIONS

AA	Archaeologia Aeliana
BRAND	History of Newcastle (2 vols)
END	Early Newcastle Deeds (Surtees Society vol 137)
GROSS	The Gild Merchant (2 vols)
NRS	Newcastle Records Series
PRO	Public Records Office

CHAPTER I

The origins of the Freemen

The Freemen, or Burgesses[1], of Newcastle first appear in documentary records in the twelfth century. There can be no doubt they were in existence long before that time, but the evidence is inferential rather than direct, so an element of speculation necessarily comes into any attempt to find the origin of the institution.

The status of burgess-ship is a legal concept (the burgess being distinguished from others by the possession of rights, privileges and obligations which were attached to the status) and it is fortunate that a document dating from the reign of Stephen is still in existence setting out the customs of the Burgesses of Newcastle in the reign of Henry I[2]. It is not appropriate to explore these customs here – all we need note for the moment is that examination of them has shown that they have diverse origins, some Celtic (i.e. ancient British), some Danish, some Anglo-Saxon, some even perhaps Roman. This illustrates the various strands in the early history of the town which probably originated as a civil settlement of Romano-British population outside the Roman fort known to us as Pons Aelius, and continued through the Anglian, Danish and Norman invasions until we get our first real knowledge of it late in the eleventh century when the castle was founded[3]. We may thus look for the origins of the Burgesses in the organisations of (a) the Anglo Saxons (b) the Danes (c) the British and (d) the Romans.

(a) The Anglo-Saxons

Stubbs considered that virtually all our civic institutions were derived from the Germanic tribes who migrated to England from the late fourth century onwards. He found evidence of

---

[1] As to the identity of Freemen and Burgesses see Appendix 1.

[2] Appendix 2.

[3] Robert son of William the Conqueror founded or refounded the New Castle in 1080. It is assumed to have been of the "motte and bailey" type, constructed of wood, replaced by stone during the 12th century.

1

their early civic organisation in the works of Caesar and Tacitus, and traced their evolution from then onwards. Such derivation is, in general, probably correct but it does not account for the Burgesses of Newcastle having customary laws which were in some cases directly contrary to the laws of the Anglo Saxons, whilst at the same time having laws which appear to be derived from British sources, and others which have a suggestion of Roman origin. This indicates that while Anglo-Saxon law and custom no doubt played their part in the development of the institution we must look elsewhere for its origin.

(b) The Danes

From the latter part of the eighth century until the late eleventh century the Danes and Vikings attacked, settled in and occupied large parts of England, particularly in the East, from the Thames to South Durham. The area now called Northumberland suffered many attacks, but would seem to have been virtually free from settlement or permanent occupation by the Danes. Evidence for the detailed history of the area during the Danish period is scanty and remains to be fully investigated, but it seems probable that Northumberland under the ancient Kings and later Earls who were their successors, managed to maintain independence of the Danes to a very great degree. If we are correct in believing that Newcastle was in the seventh century the "famous royal town" referred to by Bede as Ad Murum (which can only be located elsewhere by ignoring or perverting Bede's own description) we cannot seek the origin of the Burgesses in a Danish context, and we may well think the town's status as a borough arose through its being fortified against the Danes. This is perhaps borne out by the fact that amongst the twelfth century customs there is only one (relating to the settlement of merchants' disputes) which may have a Danish or Scandinavian origin. Had the origins of the Burgesses stemmed from Scandinavia one would have expected to find a stronger Scandinavian element than this amongst their laws.

(c) The British

In fairly sharp distinction to the last paragraph, we find in the customs of Newcastle strong evidence of affinity with the early laws of Wales and Ireland. This suggests that the Burgesses must have one of their major roots in a Celtic (i.e. British) system. Bearing in mind that a large part of the population of Lothian migrated to Wales about the end of the Roman period, and that they were of the tribe of Votadini who occupied the area stretching from the Tyne or perhaps the Tees to the Forth, we may well see a common origin in the similarities of Newcastle customs and Welsh laws. It is of even greater interest to find similarities with early Irish law, for the Irish sprang from an earlier Celtic immigration than the Welsh, and this suggests that the Votadini may themselves have had a common origin with the earlier Celts rather than the later branch. Be this as it may, it does not seem entirely unreasonable to suggest a British origin for the Burgesses.

(d) The Romans

It has been usually considered up to fairly recent years that when the Roman legions were withdrawn from Britain Roman civilisation collapsed and disappeared. Recent archaeological investigations seem, however, to show that there was continuity of occupation in some of the Roman towns, and that many Roman buildings (and particularly defensive walls) remained in existence for centuries after the legions departed. The immigrant Angles and Saxons no doubt brought their own language and customs to places where they settled, but it does not follow that local laws and usages were displaced. Roman law and the Roman legal system did very largely disappear in England, and it may be surprising to find traces of what look like Roman law in the Newcastle customs of some seven centuries later. Such traces do nevertheless appear, and although it is impossible to prove any kind of Roman origin for the civic system of the Burgesses in the twelfth century, it still remains a possibility that one of their roots may go back to this source.

One thing however is important in considering the question of origins, and this is the free status of the Burgesses, of which the twelfth century customs provide ample evidence. Status in that age was a matter of very great importance; the status of a free man was no accident, depending as it did on free birth (or manumission out of slavery, though the freed man was of lower standing than the man born free), and it carried obligations as well as privileges – in particular the privilege of bearing arms, and the duty of using them to defend the town against enemies. These were redefined by Henry II's Assize of Arms 1181 and still today the admission oath paper of a Freeman of Newcastle bears the words "and stands charged with a musket for the defence of the Town".

This free status of the Burgesses is emphasised in the custom that there was no merchet heriot blodwite or stengesdint in the town[4]. The absence of merchet and heriot, both of which were well known to the British and Danes, seems to suggest that the origin of the freedom is not to be found in the legal systems of these races. Similarly the freedom from blodwite and stengesdint suggests that the Anglo Saxon system cannot have given rise to the Burgesses' custom. This leaves us with the Romans as its originators – and the Romans knew none of these things. It is possible, though certainly not provable, that the free status of the Burgesses stems from the freedom of the Roman provincial citizen, or the retired Roman soldier who settled, perhaps with a British wife, in the civil settlement attached to the Roman fort above Hadrian's bridge over the Tyne.

The customs also show, by inference, that Newcastle had its borough court, which held its three principal meetings at Michaelmas, Christmas and Easter. This borough court was not only judicial but also administrative, the governing body of the town, being in fact the ancient folk moot of the Anglo Saxon system, administering the general law as varied by the old established local customs (which were recorded because they were variations). It can thus be seen that the Burgesses' legal institutions reflect the political history of the town, as indeed might be expected, containing strands of Roman, British and Anglian law with a very small accretion of Danish and one very recent Norman innovation. Of these strands the British and

---

[4] Merchet and heriot payments due to feudal superiors on the marriage of a daughter, and on death. Blodwite and stengesdint were fines for causing bloodshed and assault.

the Anglian are clearly the principal, and they seem fairly equal in content. It is noticeable that the method of commencing proceedings, and the rules as to who could be admitted to the burgess-ship, are British, whilst those as to the jurisdiction of the court are Anglian: and the possible traces of Roman law occur in conjunction with the customs of British origin, not those of Anglian. This again might be expected on *a priori* grounds and is consistent with the other aspects of political and legal history. The evidence we have as to the origins of the Burgesses can thus be seen to be inconclusive, but such as it is seems to point to an early origin, based perhaps on a Roman-British system, nurtured and developed by the Anglian system superimposed upon it, and becoming firmly established probably during that golden period of Northumbrian history when the Kingdom stretched from the Forth to the Humber and from the eastern sea to the western: when Northumbria led the western world in civilisation: and when the town later to become Newcastle could be described by Bede as "the famous Royal town".

CHAPTER 2

The Municipal History of the Freemen

Numerous histories of Newcastle have been written showing the development of the town, often with much detail. Many of these histories refer to the Freemen only in passing whilst others hardly mention them at all. The object of this chapter is therefore to sketch the history of the Freemen as the principal organisation of the town in order to illustrate not only their continuity but also the rise and fall of their importance over the centuries.

It must be understood that, to a very large extent, the history of the town is the history of the Freemen. From before the Conquest up to the nineteenth century virtually nothing of importance happened in the town or its affairs in which the Freemen were not directly involved or for which they were not responsible. In any community over a long period its history must have many different aspects, and Newcastle is no exception; there are many aspects of various events which between them throw light on the history of the Freemen. Some of these can be looked at separately but there are two so closely interwoven that they cannot really be isolated; when considering one the other is essential to provide explanations or background, without which proper understanding becomes impossible. These two aspects are respectively the political or local government aspect and the commercial or trade aspect. The word "commercial" is here used to cover not only wholesale and retail trade both home and foreign, but also the provision of goods and services by craftsmen. All town traders and craftsmen great and small were obliged during at least six centuries of the Middle Ages to be Freemen - unless so qualified they were not permitted by law to trade. This dichotomy of the Freemen's interests must be constantly borne in mind: it is a key to understanding many events otherwise obscure.

We have no direct evidence concerning the Burgesses before the record of their customs in the reign of Henry I, though analysis of the customs, coupled with the general history of the town, can tell us something of their earlier existence. The customs at this time show us a community of Burgesses who are Freemen (i.e. not villeins, bondmen or serfs) carrying on trades particularly in skins, corn and woollen cloth, whose chief official was the Provost (praepositus). They already had a privileged status and liabilities in relation to non-Burgesses and a body of special local customary law to regulate their affairs in the borough court. The Provost, although a royal official governing the town for the King (who was Lord of the borough), was elected annually. The borough court held three principal meetings each year (at Michaelmas, Christmas and Easter) at which the town's government was carried on, in this respect following the law laid down by King Edgar, and being the successor of the Anglo-Saxon folk moot of the town. It was the duty of all Burgesses to attend. The list of tolls[1] attached to the customs shows that extensive trade was being conducted: some of the customs also indicate that the Burgesses were already carrying on some trades as a collective or corporate body. Although there was not yet any legal concept of an incorporated community of Burgesses, gilds or fraternities for social or trade purposes were well known in practice. The customs form a continuous connecting link through generation after generation of Freemen even to the present day and underlie many of the later disputes in the municipal affairs of the town.

In 1168 we find the Burgesses in trouble: they had insisted on applying the old fashioned or obsolete legal procedure known as compurgation to a Knight, and were fined twenty marks for their failure to adapt themselves to Norman ways. This provides an illustration of the Burgesses as a collective body: each burgess would have to contribute his share of the fine and the Provost would have to arrange for its collection and payment to the Sheriff of the County.

The first Royal Charter to the Burgesses of Newcastle was that of Henry II in 1175 by which he granted them freedom from toll throughout all his lands.[2] This was a commercial

---

[1] See Acts of the Parliament of Scotland vol 1 p33 or Brand II pp130,131.

[2] AA 4th series XII p260.

privilege of very considerable value and again demonstrated the fact that the Burgesses were recognised as an organised body. The next important grants were from King John who granted them the "farm" of the Borough in perpetuity at the fixed fee of £60, later raised to £100 per annum. This meant that the Burgesses would pay a fixed rent direct to the Royal Exchequer, instead of the Sheriff of Northumberland paying a fixed amount to the exchequer and profiting by collecting what he could in rents, tolls or charges from the Burgesses individually. Freedom from the interference of the Sheriff in this respect was a very valuable privilege to the Burgesses, but the grant also shows that the royal officials were prepared to accept the Burgesses as a responsible body who could be relied upon to pay the fixed rent. At later times adverse circumstances, such as the Scottish wars, sometimes affected the ability of the Burgesses to pay. It was on occasions remitted but this payment of £100 continued annually until 1870 before it was finally abolished.

In 1216 came another very important step. The Burgesses were able to obtain from King John a Charter which included the right to have a Gild Merchant and to use some of the customs of Winchester. In later ages the use of a common seal, the grant of the farm of the borough or the grant of a Gild Merchant, were considered in law to have effected the incorporation of the Burgesses as a legal body. This illustrates the importance of these steps. Although the Burgesses of Newcastle were not formally incorporated until 1189 by a Charter of Queen Elizabeth, they were treated from the early twelfth century onwards as having been incorporated. We do not know when a common seal was first used but one appears about 1223.

Up to this time the town had been governed by the Burgesses meeting in their Borough Court, under the Provost. A few days after King John granted his Charter to the Burgesses in 1216 he wrote a letter to the current Provost (Daniel son of Nicholas) under the name of Mayor. The name Provost, however, did not drop out of use immediately and the word Mayor (a foreign and suspected title) only came in gradually over quite a long period. It seems to have been well established by about 1250, although it was challenged again at the end of the century, as a result of which the Mayor was for a time known as the Chief Bailiff.

Edward I by charter in 1299 extended the town boundaries by granting to the Burgesses that part of the manor of Pandon which lay in Byker adjoining the old Newcastle boundary.[3] The charter states that it is for the improvement and security of Newcastle (i.e. military reasons) - to enable the town wall then being built to exclude enemies from the area of high ground from which they might otherwise dominate the low land known as "Pandon in Newcastle". The charter does not mention the Gild Merchant but does provide that no loading or unloading as such should be carried on in Pandon without the approval of the Burgesses.

The function of the Gild Merchant (into which all Burgesses were entitled to admission) was not the government of the town but the control of the trading activities of the Burgesses both collective and individual. In practice it would without doubt come under the influence and control of the principal traders, who being also the principal townsmen, would in the latter capacity also influence and control the affairs of the town. This continued to be governed by the meeting of the Burgesses under their Mayor. During the thirteenth century the principal Burgesses formed themselves into an exclusive gild, claiming for its members alone the benefit of the Burgesses' trading privileges and to exclude the lesser Burgesses from membership. The Gild members used or abused the powers of town government to oppress the lesser Burgesses. This is established by the fairly full report of a legal action taken in 1305 by "certain poor Burgesses on behalf of themselves and other poor Burgesses" against "the rich Burgesses of the gild merchant". The case was heard in the Exchequer Court where judgment was given for £50 damages

---

[3] It may be of interest to note that although the charter expressly relates to Pandon in Byker it is commonly referred to as if it related to the whole of Pandon. This appears to be incorrect as part of Pandon was within the ancient east boundary of the town. See Brand II p146 and Surtees Society vol 137 p79 (No 113) and note on p80.

(a very large sum) against the rich Burgesses. The court found expressly that all the Burgesses of Newcastle, both rich and poor, were equally entitled to trade freely and quietly and without oppression in the town (see Appendix 3).

No mention appears in the Exchequer court case of any trade or craft companies in Newcastle. If not already existing, such companies must have been formed during the next quarter century or so, for twelve companies appear by name in 1342 as being the best and most respectable (perhaps also the largest) companies, which implies that there were others. It can be inferred from events in 1342 that although the rich Burgesses had been defeated in 1305, they had not changed their ways. They had in fact continued to control the town to the disadvantage of the remaining Burgesses and indeed had misgoverned it for their own advantage. Edward III is said to have reorganised the municipal aspect of the Freemen in 1334[4] but there had been internal trouble in the town for some years and it continued. Discontent came to a head in a meeting held on the Friday before St Valentine's Day 1342, when the full Gild (i.e. Mayor and Burgesses as the governing body of the town) met in the Hospital of St Mary the Virgin and agreed upon new articles of government,[5] the contents of which are very revealing. The fact of the meeting itself demonstrates that the government of the town was still legally in the hands of the Burgesses as a whole, rather than in any smaller select body or gild. No Gild Merchant is mentioned. The articles are concerned principally to correct administration of the town with regard to finance and justice, but the second article reaffirmed the right of every burgess, whether poor or rich and of whatever condition, to go on board all ships coming to the town, belonging to a burgess or a foreigner, and to purchase whatever merchandise, victuals or cargo he might require. It further confirmed the right of Burgesses to participate in wholesale or collective bargains. This article clearly derives from the Burgesses' recorded ancient customs and the 1305 lawsuit. Another article places the election of the Mayor and

[4] Brand II p154.

[5] Brand II p155.

other officials in the hands of twenty-four Burgesses, two from each of the twelve most respectable of the trade companies of the town. The twelve companies specified, then or later known as the misteries (commonly misspelt "mysteries"), were the Wool Merchants, Mercers, Skinners, Tailors, Saddlers, Corn Merchants, Bakers, Tanners, Cordwainers, Butchers, Smiths and Fullers. The articles were confirmed by the King on 20th October 1342, but trouble between the two factions continued, culminating in the death of the Mayor, John of Denton (who was probably the leader of the magnates and the principal cause of the complaints), after which the provisions for the election of the Mayor were called in by the King for revocation. In 1345 the 1342 method of election was cancelled and a new system instituted. This placed the election of Mayor and other officers under the control of the greater rather than the lesser Burgesses. The remaining provisions, however, were not cancelled. The elections continued to be a source of trouble and upon the petition of the Burgesses in 1371 the whole of the articles of 1342 were reconfirmed by the King; they were again confirmed by Richard II in 1378 and then by successive sovereigns down to Elizabeth. The Mayor and Burgesses in Gild assembled in fact remained the official governing body of the town even after the charter of James I, which continued their powers but placed restrictions upon them. These in effect gave control of the town's affairs to the Common Council which had been set up about the middle of the sixteenth century.

Numerous further privileges were granted to the Burgesses during the fifteenth century. We may notice in particular the charter of Henry IV in 1400 whereby the town of Newcastle was separated from the County of Northumberland and made a County of itself with its own Sheriff and a body of six Aldermen to act as Justices of the Peace. The Mayor and all other civic officials were drawn from and elected by the Burgesses, though the leading Burgesses would almost certainly have a controlling interest in the elections.

There is evidence that in 1438 further trouble, of the same kind as in 1305 and 1342, occurred again. The Mayor and

Aldermen as plaintiffs in the Star Chamber proceedings of 1515 (referred to below) said they could produce an old book of articles of a common Gild held in 1438 (17 Henry VI) recording variances and discord between "merchants of this Gild and craftsmen of the same Gild" and a declaration and agreement of the common Gild regulating the sale of goods from ships. Builders of ships and houses were to have the first preference to buy goods required for their trades. Merchants came next with regard to their merchandise and then every craftsman could purchase reasonably for his own sustentation and use in his house and not to sell again to strangers. It is noticeable that merchants were differentiated from craftsmen but both were members of the same Gild and the decision seems to be a somewhat twisted version of the second article of 1342. It probably indicates a stage where the members of the merchant companies were separating themselves from the craft companies, and the merchants were claiming for themselves the exclusive benefit of the Merchant Gild. They had a separate meeting hall in the upper floor of the building erected by Roger Thornton in 1412 as a Hospital or Almshouse (known as Thornton's Hospital, otherwise the Maison Dieu), which was situated adjoining the east end of the Guildhall. This was demolished in 1823 but rebuilt containing the Merchant Adventurers' court in precisely the same position, to which the ornaments and furnishing of the old Merchants' meeting hall were transferred.

We do not know precisely when the Merchants separated themselves, at least in part, from the remaining companies, perhaps even before Roger Thornton's death in 1429, but in 1477 occur the first records of an already existing "fellowship of merchants" which consisted primarily of merchants who were members of the Drapers (wool merchants) the Boothmen (corn merchants) and the Mercers (retailers of miscellaneous smallwares), companies all of which had existed from before 1342. There are also shadowy traces in the Merchants' records of a company of Grocers and Spicers which was probably absorbed by the Mercers and the fellowship may also have included a separate fraternity of Hostmen (coal merchants) first recorded in 1515 as already existing. This fellowship of Merchants later claimed to be the Gild Merchant established under the charter of King John,[6] though when all the circumstances are examined, it would seem that such a claim is of doubtful validity.

In 1515 trouble between the lesser Burgesses and the Merchants broke out again, apparently for the same reasons as before, namely that the Merchants were endeavouring to abuse their power or influence as the principal governors and magistrates of the town, to prevent the lesser Burgesses trading freely. Threats, or alleged threats, of violence by the lesser Freemen (whose leader was alleged to have exclaimed "we bin as good men as they who in former times slew and killed their Mayor") so frightened the Mayor and Aldermen that the Gild Day was not kept. They petitioned the King who referred it to the Court of Star Chamber. A commission of enquiry was then set up by the Court, a very high-powered state tribunal for constitutional and administrative matters, giving decisions which were political as well as judicial or legal. The King personally attended the court when judgement was given in this case.

Conflicting evidence was given by considerable numbers of witnesses on both sides. The lesser Freemen, who called themselves the Gild Merchants, asserted that they had traded freely and without interference from time out of mind, whilst the Merchants asserted that whenever they found anyone trading without licence from them he was prosecuted and fined. The Merchants did not mention membership or even the existence of the Gild Merchant, though they did claim exclusive rights of trading within their own spheres. The court settled the matter by a decree which was in effect a masterly compromise. It laid down that no-one could carry on any of the trades of the Merchants without their licence but that any Burgess wishing to join one of the Merchant companies should be permitted to do so. Burgesses with insufficient means could be excluded and those with adequate means were to pay admission fees reflecting their financial status. This could be

---

[6] Surtess Society vol 101 pp110 et seq.

claimed as a victory for both sides and virtually restored the position to what it had been three centuries before.

Whatever the internal troubles of the Freemen may have been, as a whole they were completely predominant in town affairs. They formed the governing body of the town: official positions were open only to Freemen and only Freemen had any voice, even if somewhat indirect, in elections. Virtually every townsman from semi-skilled artisan up to merchant prince was obliged to be a Freeman, as otherwise he could not carry on his trade or craft. It must also be remembered that very large parts of the thirteenth, fourteenth, and fifteenth centuries were spent at war with Scotland. In addition to any other functions the Freemen were the men who manned the walls and kept watch and ward against the Scots, whose army or marauding parties might attack at almost any time. Despite these wars, the trade of the town had increased greatly. The wool trade, in which fortunes had been made in the fourteenth and fifteenth centuries, declined but the coal trade had increased and with it not only the profits of coal mining and trading but also benefits in shipping, ship building and numerous other trades. The Freemen controlled the Port of Tyne from the river mouth to Hedwin Streams (near Heddon-on-the-Wall) and as, for fiscal reasons, all trade had to be channelled through Newcastle, this brought considerable advantages. It is probably reasonable to say that in the seventeenth century the Freemen were at the peak of their trading power. Thereafter it began to decline, at first slowly but in the late seventeenth and eighteenth centuries more and more rapidly.

Following the Star Chamber case of 1515, the affairs of the Freemen must be seen for the rest of the sixteenth century against the background of the religious, national and international events and politics which stirred all England during the reigns of Henry VIII, Edward VI, Mary and Elizabeth. It was a period of great and comparatively rapid change, not only nationally but also locally. This period is marked by the rise of the Merchants' and the Hostmen's companies, who managed to acquire effective if not full legal control of the government of the town. It must of course be remembered that as in earlier centuries this was a matter of the same persons having power in both the political aspect of the town's development and also in its commercial affairs. It can best be described by saying that the town was being governed by the principal business men of the day.

The Hostmen's Company formed probably after 1439[7] is first referred to in the records of the Star Chamber Case, though it must have been in existence for quite some time before, as one of the witnesses gave evidence that he was a member of that company and had acted as one of its stewards. By the end of the century when the Fraternity of Hostmen was formally incorporated by the town's Great Charter from Queen Elizabeth, they had reached a position where the forty-nine persons named as members of the Company included the Mayor, all ten Aldermen, five Councillors, two Coroners and the Town Clerk, and no less than twenty-five, then or later, served as Mayor, Sheriff or Alderman. The Fellowship of Merchants (which continued to consist of the Drapers, Boothmen and Mercers, operating as distinct branches within the fellowship) obtained from Edward VI in 1546 a charter incorporating the Merchant Adventurers' Company. This consisted not of all the Fellowship of Merchants but of those Merchant Adventurers in Newcastle who were members of the "Fellowship of Merchant Adventurers in Brabant in the parts of Beyond the Seas", i.e. those merchants who were trading in the Netherlands. This new Company was authorised to admit to membership any of the subjects of the King or his successors dwelling in Newcastle.[8] It was not expressly laid down that membership was restricted to Freemen, though this was the case because no-one but a Freeman could carry on trade. The new Merchant Adventurers' Company almost at once began to admit members of the Drapers, Boothmen and Mercers Companies and their apprentices. The Fellowship of Merchants thus merged into the new company of Merchant

---

[7] Deudy on the Records of the Hostmen's Company - Surtees Society vol 105 p XXII quoting Statute 18 Hen VI cap 4.

[8] Surtees Society vol 93 p287.

Adventurers. The older companies of Drapers, Boothmen and Mercers had a specific part to play in the annual elections and thus maintained a theoretical separate existence until this function disappeared in 1835, since when they have lost their separate identities. It seems clear that during the sixteenth and seventeenth centuries the Merchant Adventurers' and Hostmen's Companies virtually controlled the entire commerce of the town and it can therefore be said that the Freemen at this period governed the town civically, politically and commercially. And it must not be forgotten that they were still responsible for its military defence.

The organisation of local government also began to change during this period. It is by no means clear when the Common Council of the town was first instituted. The 1342 Articles of Government had decreed that twenty-four Burgesses drawn from the twelve most reputable and important Freemen's companies should be primarily responsible for the election of the Mayor and officials. It may be that this body of twenty-four electors developed into some form of governing committee of the Mayor and Burgesses. The first Sheriff was appointed (to replace the Bailiffs) in 1400 when Newcastle became a county of itself and at the same time six Aldermen were appointed to act as Justices of the Peace. The number of Aldermen was increased from six to ten by charter in 1557. In the same year a decree of the Privy Council regulating various matters in Newcastle ordered that the twenty-four electors should be assistants to the Mayor and Aldermen, and were to be the Common Council of the town for the ensuing year. This seems to be the official inception of the Common Council, though some organisation of the kind may well have been in operation earlier. The same decree ordered that the Common Seal of the town should not be affixed to any document without the assent of the Mayor, Aldermen, Sheriff and Common Council: clearly a considerable change from the governance of the town by the Mayor and Burgesses in full Gild. This decree was followed in 1561 by another decree made by the Lord President of the Council of the North "for the better government of Newcastle" to the effect that the ten Aldermen should be continued and with the Mayor and Sheriff should be the chief rulers and magistrates of the town and that the twenty-four electors should remain the Common Council of the town over and beside the ten Aldermen. This suggests a transfer of power from the general meeting of Burgesses to the body later known as the Corporation, which although consisting entirely of Freemen became, through a complicated electoral system, virtually self-electing, as indeed the decree of the Star Chamber in 1515 may have intended. In 1589 Queen Elizabeth granted a charter to the Burgesses whereby they were for the first time officially incorporated (up to this time they had been treated as a legal corporation by successive sovereigns and national governments, but could claim to be incorporated only by prescription or implication). This charter granted to the Mayor and Burgesses assembled together, full authority and power to rule the town. It further authorised either the Mayor and Burgesses and the Common Council (i.e. the Mayor, the Sheriff, ten Aldermen and twenty-four council men), or the Mayor and Burgesses assembled, to impose fines, punishments or imprisonment to secure the better observance of the bye-laws. Thus the power of making bye-laws was given to the Mayor and Burgesses, but enforcement was authorised either by the Mayor and Burgesses or by the Common Council.[9] This appears to be, if not the origin, at least the earliest recognition of the system of dual control which still remains in relation to the Town Moor.

Such a system of local government was not satisfactory for a prosperous and expanding town. The principal Freemen, the most influential of whom were comprised in the Mayor, Sheriff, Aldermen and Common Council, therefore set to work to obtain a new charter from the Crown. They went to considerable trouble and expense in this and were successful in obtaining a charter in 1600 from Queen Elizabeth, usually known as the Great Charter. This repeated the provisions of the earlier charter in greater detail, but with some apparently slight variations which, however, were more important than was at first apparent. It declared that the Mayor, Sheriff, Aldermen

---

[9] Brand II pp597,8

and twenty-four Burgesses should at all future times form the Common Council of the town and gave power to the Common Council, or alternatively to the Mayor and Burgesses assembled, to make bye-laws for the government of the town, thus placing the new governing body (the Common Council) on an equal footing with the old governing body (The Mayor and Burgesses). The method of electing the Mayor and officials was again reorganised without making any real difference and the promoters of the charter took the opportunity to include in it provisions for the regulation of the town's Grammar School (now the Royal Grammar School) which became an incorporated body in its own right, but was effectively under the control of the town's corporate body. The opportunity was also taken (indeed this may have been one of the main objects of obtaining the charter) to incorporate the Fraternity of Hostmen which included the Mayor and most of the principal merchants who were of course all Freemen. The Great Charter is sometimes seen as a deliberate and successful effort by the principal Freemen to secure for themselves not only the government of the town, but also of the very lucrative coal trade, and at the same time to set up a school for the education of their children in order to perpetuate these advantages. The opposite view is that the controlling body in the town was with a great sense of responsiblity securing the provision of arrangements which were intended to give the town good and stable government, together with a soundly based and well controlled commerce which would provide prosperity for all the Freemen and their families (remembering in this connection that virtually all townsmen of any standing were Freemen). Both of these views may have some element of truth in them, but neither can be accepted without considerable caution.

Queen Elizabeth died in 1603 and in accordance with the usual practice of those times it was considered necessary to obtain confirmation or a fresh charter from her successor James I. This was accordingly obtained in 1604. The new charter repeated the powers and provisions of the Great Charter in virtually the same words, but again slightly amended the system of elections in form though not in substance. It also added an important provision similar to that of the earlier decree of the Council of the North that acts of the Mayor and Burgesses purporting to dispose of any of the town's properties or money should be void unless made with the consent of, and in the presence of, the Mayor and the rest of the Common Council, or by a majority of them, and that the Common Seal of the town should not be appended to any documents without similar consent. The effect of this was that, although the power of the Mayor and Burgesses in Gild assembled (now usually known as the Court of Guild) was not taken away, it was subjected in virtually all important matters to the control of the Common Council. From this time onwards the Court of Guild exercised its power and acted in the government of the town only on rare occasions - so rarely in fact that it could later be contended that the powers no longer existed, ignoring the provision in the charter that the powers should not cease because of non-user. This question became acute in 1830 when the Stewards of the Freemen's Companies obtained the opinion of two eminent counsel, both of whom advised that the powers were still in existence. These two charters, namely those of 1600 and 1604, were known as the Governing Charters and Newcastle was governed by Freemen under their provisions until the Municipal Corporations Act 1835 destroyed the Freemen's powers (both of the Court of Guild and the Common Council) so far as local government affairs were concerned.

The reigns of James I and Charles I are not remarkable for domestic events in the municipal history of the Freemen. In 1629 there was an official enquiry into the rights and privileges of the Freemen as a corporate body. The Attorney General, acting for the Crown, examined the various Acts of Parliament, Charters, writs, records and ancient books of the Corporation and heard witnesses. The Court of King's Bench thereafter gave judgement upholding the rights and powers as claimed. In 1644 the Freemen under Sir John Marley held the town for King Charles against the Scots army but were finally forced to capitulate. During the period under Cromwell there was some political manoeuvring but in general the Freemen preferred to accept the government for the time being and to make the maintenance of their chartered rights the main object of their policy. This policy might be considered somewhat negative but it was successful in that while many boroughs were constantly interfered with by the Cromwellian government, Newcastle emerged at the Restoration in much the same condition as it had been prior to the Civil War. Charles II confirmed the Governing Charters in 1664, though ordering that the appointment of a Recorder and Town Clerk should be approved by him. In the period before the Revolution of 1688 there was again a good deal of political manoeuvring, but ultimately all James II's interference with charters was declared void. The civic authority appointed under James II was immediately ejected and a new body of civic officials elected. The Freemen were thus restored to their ancient liberties.

In the eighteenth century public opinion and the law turned slowly but effectively against the rights and powers of the Freemen's companies to exclude non-Freemen from their various trades.[10] These rights were not formally abolished until 1836 when the Municipal Corporation Act came into force but by this time they had virtually disappeared.

During the seventeenth and eighteenth centuries the Common Council developed into what was virtually a self-electing hierarchy, drawn very largely from the Merchant Adventurers' and Hostmen's companies. The Common Council became more and more the government of the town. The Courts of Guild continued to be held as before but these meetings of "the Mayor and Burgesses in Guild assembled" exerted less influence, so much so in fact that the Council became known as "the governing part of the Corporation."[11] It could be and was alleged that the Guild meetings had no power and were carried on only for the purpose of allowing the Freemen, through the stewards and their companies, an opportunity to object to the admission of apprentices or others who were thought not properly qualified. The Guild meetings

---

[10] Surtees Society vol 93 ppxii & 255.

[11] Brown, Short Account of the Freemen, Newcastle 1823, p13.

did however enable individual Freemen to voice grievances and thus exercised some restraining influence on the actions of the Common Council. The latter part of the eighteenth century was a period when many boroughs became corrupt, but there seems to have been comparatively little corruption in Newcastle municipal affairs. This may well have been due to the existence of the dual control. The action of the Stewards of the Companies in 1771, which ultimately resulted in the Town Moor Act 1774, is a good example. The politics of this period and in the years leading up to the Municipal Corporations Act 1835 were confused, but it seems clear that the Common Council pursued a course of moderate and generally satisfactory conduct of the town's affairs. An official enquiry by Parliamentary Commissioners into the local government of the town, held during October and November 1833, revealed only a few comparatively minor complaints. Although there were a few dissident voices, the report of the proceedings[12] does seem to show that the town's government was neither very corrupt nor inefficient.

The destruction of the Freemen's powers of local government by the Municipal Corporations Act in 1836 might seem a logical point at which to end this narrative of their municipal history, but this is not wholly true. The Act preserved the Freemen and their rights so far as they were not inconsistent with the Act's provisions. In particular the Act did not affect the rights of the resident Freemen and widows of Freemen to graze cows on the Town Moor, in accordance with the ancient rights confirmed by the Town Moor Act 1774. These rights in effect gave them control over the surface of the Moor which was a matter of concern to some members of the new local authority, and to this extent the Freemen had a continuing interest and influence in this part of Newcastle's municipal affairs.

During the century and a half since 1836 the Freemen have had a relationship, sometimes harmonious and at other times inharmonious, with the Town Council, but this relationship has been based on the problems arising in connection with

---

[12] Verbatim transcript published by Newcastle Journal 15th Jan, 1834.

Town Moor lands. It therefore seems appropriate to include this part of the Freemen's history in a separate chapter on the Town Moor.

CHAPTER 3

The Gild Merchant
of Newcastle upon Tyne

The Gild Merchant of Newcastle upon Tyne has been mentioned in greater or less detail in many histories of the town and in studies of particular events, but no full account of its rise and decline and its survival into the present time has yet been given. Indeed events previously overlooked have shown that in the past some ideas of Newcastle domestic history have been distorted by misunderstanding of the evidence then known.

Before entering upon this account it is necessary for us, living in the latter part of the twentieth century, to adjust our minds to the atmosphere of the early middle ages. We who for some two centuries or more have taken very much for granted the freedom of individual citizens to trade must, in the context of the Gild Merchant, appreciate that this principle is comparatively modern. In the early Middle Ages there was little democracy and the government of the country was almost completely authoritarian, though restrained by the strength of customary laws and the practical difficulties of enforcing decrees which were not generally acceptable. In those days anyone who wished to carry on a trade had to be able to show that he was entitled to do so. In the chartered towns or boroughs, the right to trade in most cases depended upon membership of a group privileged either by ancient custom or by Charter of the King or a feudal superior. The right to hold a market or fair, a valuable franchise, could be granted only by the King or one of the greater feudal barons: foreign, that is to say non-local, traders were regarded with suspicion and were only allowed to trade with permission granted by a local official. Another important factor to be remembered is that it was necessary for everyone to be part of some recognised organisation. In rural areas this was the Manor wherein the Lord had personal as well as territorial jurisdiction. The tenants derived their status from their membership, in whatever capacity, as tenants of that Manor. In the towns the organisation was either the community of Burgesses as a whole, or perhaps within that community membership of a smaller Gild existing for a particular purpose, trade or craft: thus a member of say a Tanners' Gild (who would be a member either because his father had been a member or because he had been trained or introduced by some other member and accepted) was permitted to carry on the craft of tanning; the Gild would take steps to ensure that no stranger set up in business as a tanner in the town without the consent of the Gild. This form of social system in relation to trade persisted right through the Middle Ages and into, if not beyond, the eighteenth century. We in the twentieth century also take for granted the increasingly easy and rapid forms of transport and communication which have come into existence during the past two centuries. In the medieval period transport and communication were cumbersome, slow and difficult. This had the effect of insulating towns from each other, making them very parochial in their outlook. The resulting hostility between towns led their Burgesses to take up restrictive attitudes by which they attempted to retain all local trade in their own hands. Such policies proved disastrous for many towns as the trade went elsewhere. The restrictions had to be relaxed, at least temporarily, but after a time were often reintroduced.

Another aspect of life in early and later medieval times was the system of community trading or common bargains. By this system a member of a Gild had to share his purchases of goods with his fellow members at cost price. The customs of the Burgesses of Newcastle in the time of Henry I seem to suggest in a number of cases that common trade was being carried on. They also show that certain trades could be carried on only by Burgesses, and further that certain fairly onerous tolls were charged on imports and exports from the town, whose jurisdiction even then extended from Tynemouth as far as the head of the tidal waters of the Tyne at a point known as Hedwin Streams (between Ryton and Heddon). It may be that the Burgesses themselves were already exempt from these tolls as they certainly were later. They were liable to contribute to all the financial burdens of the town and would endeavour to recover at least part of these burdens by charging tolls against the goods of non-Burgesses. A similar position would arise in other boroughs where Newcastle traders would have to pay full toll on their goods from which the local Burgesses would be exempt. During the reign of Henry II the Burgesses of many towns were exempted from such tolls everywhere and in fact Henry II granted a Charter to the Burgesses of Newcastle in 1175 confirming their exemption from "toll and passage and pontage and from the hanse and from all other customs throughout all my lands"[1] (an expression which would seem to include his French lands as well as English). The word hanse in this context probably means the payments exacted by Gilds Merchant in other towns and the exemption suggests that the Newcastle Burgesses were being treated as members of a Gild Merchant.

King John, on 28th January 1216, issued a charter to "our Burgesses of Newcastle upon Tyne for their faithful services and unto their heirs forever" which granted or confirmed a number of privileges already enjoyed (they can be seen amongst the earlier customs and charter) and also that the Burgesses should have Gild Merchant. This has been generally accepted as the origin of Newcastle's Gild Merchant. Those who put forward the Charter of John as the origin of the Gild Merchant can at least point to the certainty of an authentic document. This, however, disregards the fact that the Burgesses had been exercising some at least of the privileges of a Gild Merchant for more than eighty years and had been free of tolls and hanse for forty years before 1216. It seems probable that the Burgesses obtained their Charter from King John to confirm an already existing trade monopoly and privileges, rather than to create one which had not previously existed. The wording of the Charter itself is consistent with this interpretation. It confirms privileges which documentary evidence shows to have been in existence in the reign of Henry I and which had probably existed for a very long period before then. As an original foundation of a Gild Merchant it is late,

---

[1] AA 4th ser. vol III p260.

such privilege having been granted to Burgesses of other towns much earlier. In some towns e.g. London, the Cinque Ports and Norwich, the Burgesses never had any such grant or confirmation, perhaps because they were so strongly established that it was unnecessary. The same could well be said of Newcastle.

The true nature and function of a Gild Merchant was much disputed and much misunderstood by the eighteenth and nineteenth century historians. This was cleared up by an American scholar, Charles Gross, in a masterly survey of the very extensive evidence[2] from which he showed that it was an official body, part of the system of government of the free boroughs, whose duty and function was the supervision of the trade, manufactures and crafts of the Burgesses. The legal conception of corporate bodies as single continuing entities, distinct from their members, did not come into the common law until the fourteenth and fifteenth centuries, being worked out over a very long period, but it was in later years held that the grant of Gild Merchant effected incorporation. At its inception the Gild Merchant usually, if not invariably, consisted of all the Burgesses of the town but in many cases it soon became the exclusive preserve of the larger traders. These being the principal, Burgesses tended also to take charge of the town government, so that in many places the town's affairs were in practice managed and governed by a body indistinguishable from the Gild Merchant, thus giving rise to the theory that the Gild was the origin of the later Common Councils. It was also considered by some historians, though controverted by others, that there was a long drawn out struggle by the trade or craft gilds to take political power and control from the Gild Merchant, though it has not been demonstrated that the Gild Merchant as such ever had any political power (other than influence) in the government of the town. These matters are inter-related with the customs already mentioned and proper understanding of the municipal history of the government of Newcastle is impossible without appreciating the details of the relationship.

---

[2] Gross, The Gild Merchant, Oxford 1890, reprinted 1927 and 1964, 34.

What if anything was done to set up or reorganise a Gild Merchant in Newcastle after the granting of the Charter in 1216 is not recorded. A record does exist showing what was done in Ipswich in 1201 when a Charter granted the Burgesses there a Gild Merchant.[3] These proceedings were very much in the nature of setting up *de novo* a borough authority for Ipswich of which the Gild Merchant was to form part. Although this demonstrates the organisation and functions of the Gild Merchant in Ipswich, it does not necessarily follow that the same action would be taken elsewhere in different circumstances, particularly where the borough authority already existed, though it is not unreasonable to assume there was some general similarity.

In 1234 Henry III confirmed the earlier Charter of John and included confirmation of the free customs which the Burgesses had used in the time of his grandfather, Henry II. The words of confirmation are formal and make no mention of a Gild Merchant nor is it referred to elsewhere in this Charter. In 1293 Edward I, who was systematically investigating the affairs of the boroughs, issued a "Quo Warranto" requiring the Burgesses to show, amongst other things, by what warrant they claimed to have a Gild Merchant and in the same year there is a casual reference to Hugh of Carliol as Alderman of the Gild of Newcastle. Alderman was the title of the official head of a Gild Merchant. The Burgesses must have been able to produce satisfactory evidence, for in the same year the King confirmed Henry III's Charter of 1234, which itself confirmed John's Charter of 1216.

In 1305 a dispute between the leading members of the Gild Merchant and other Burgesses, whom they did not recognise as members, came to a head. It seems probable that the dispute must have been continuing for some not inconsiderable time and it concerned the extent of the authority of the greater merchants. The "poor Burgesses" took legal action against the "rich Burgesses". The rich Burgesses claimed that they were a Gild Merchant by ancient custom and that the poor Burgesses were of no account and were not entitled to the privileges

---

[3] Surtees Society vol 93 pxxxii.

granted by the Charters. The rich Burgesses were, however, unable to sustain their case.[4] The court decreed that all the Burgesses could freely buy and sell individually or collectively without exception as in accordance with the liberties granted to the Burgesses by the King they were entitled to do, and that the rich Burgesses should do nothing to harm any of the Burgesses irrespective of whether they were members of the Gild or not. The court assessed the damages at £50 (a very large sum) and this sum was duly collected by the Sheriff and paid over to the poor Burgesses after deducting £10 for the court expenses. Details of the case are given in the Exchequer Court Plea Roll, a translation of which is given in Appendix III. A minor point of interest is that the formal receipt of the £40 damages is dated 17th January 1306 (old style) which was the traditional day for the Christmas Gild Meeting (i.e. the second Monday after the end of the feast of Christmas). It must remain a matter for regret that this record of the case in the Exchequer Plea Roll was not known to Gross, Stephenson, Tait or Dendy, whose views would have been materially affected by its contents.

A number of points stand out clearly from the report. First, legal process had not yet recognised the Gild Merchant as an incorporated body, having a fictional legal personality apart from its members, though it does seem to show that legal thought was tending towards such recognition. Secondly, membership of the Gild Merchant was claimed to be (though this was not upheld) distinct from the freedom of the town, i.e. although all Gildsmen must be Burgesses, some Burgesses were not Gildsmen, having been excluded. Thirdly, the situation as between the Gild Merchant and the Burgesses at large was that the Merchant Gild was attempting to claim for its members alone the benefit of the Burgesses' trading privileges and to exclude the non-Gildsmen from such privileges. Fourthly, the court's decision was very definitely in favour of the Burgesses at large. Fifthly, the matters in dispute were purely the trading

---

[4] Although expressly questioned they did not claim the benefit of King John's Charter, but relied on an alleged ancient custom, which however was held to be wholly contrary to justice and the law.

privileges of the Burgesses and not any question of power to govern the town. All (except the wine trade) are matters which are referred to in the Burgesses' customs in the reign of Henry I and the freedom from toll granted by the Charter of Henry II. This goes to confirm that the Burgesses had been exercising the trades as an organised and recognised body before the grant of King John's Charter of 1216.

The case is a landmark in the history of the Burgesses and the Gild Merchant, for not only did it decide that the Burgesses were free to trade but it also showed that the rich Burgesses, as they admitted, could not claim any special privilege entitling them to override the privileges of the Burgesses at large individually or collectively.

It is worth noting at this point that John's Charter of 1216 authorised the Burgesses to use some of the customs of Winchester. A Charter in very similar terms had been granted to the citizens of Winchester, allowing them a Gild Merchant and privileges similar in many cases to those allowed to Newcastle. Winchester, however, already had an existing Gild Merchant referred to in a Charter granted by Richard I. The fact that the two Charters to Winchester and Newcastle respectively are similar (in some cases identical) suggests that Newcastle, like Winchester, already had a Gild Merchant.

The name Gild Merchant seems very largely to disappear (except in formal confirmations of Royal Charters) after the Exchequer case. It reappears at the end of the fifteenth century in Royal licences to export wool, but although one of these refers to a Gild Merchant another refers to a Gild "of Merchants" and both would seem to have been granted to the body which was referred to by the Merchants themselves as a "fellowship of Merchants", to be discussed later.

It is noticeable that the Exchequer record of 1305 makes no reference to any trade or craft companies. It may be that none had been formed in Newcastle at that time, though they were well known elsewhere. In Berwick-upon-Tweed, for example, the craft gilds had been amalgamated into one Gild in 1248, the object of this being to prevent disputes between the individual Gilds. Craft gilds are first referred to, as already existing in Newcastle, in 1342 and must have been well established by that time. Edward III was much concerned with Newcastle in the early years of his reign and is said to have established the Mayor with authority and confirmed the election of magistrates, Merchants, Freemen and the commonalty in 1333-34, and it may be that this was a reorganisation of the local government of the town including setting up or authorisation of the craft gilds.[5]

Another change seems to have taken place about the beginning of the fourteenth century in the name used for the town court. Up to 1316 it is referred to in documents as the court or the full court (plena curia) but in the same year 1316 it is referred to as full gild (plena gilda).[6] This change of style may indicate that the rich merchants, having lost the case in 1305, abandonded the expression Gild Merchant and instead transferred its functions to the full gild where they could exercise authority under a different hat. Newcastle would thus have reversed the procedure of Berwick, where the craft gilds had been merged into one common Gild, but in Newcastle the Gild Merchant was divided into the craft gilds, though without destroying the Gild Merchant. It seems probable that the merchants had, from very early times in the town's history, considered themselves superior to the artificers and craftsmen. This was evidently so in 1305 and the same attitude is apparent in the evidence given to the Star Chamber in 1515 by the "Mayor, Aldermen and other honest persons of the town" relating to variance and discord in 1438-39 between "merchants of the common gild and craftsmen of the same gild", referring to "craftsmen that work of their handcraft" as compared with a "merchant that useth no other craft but merchandise".[7]

The events of 1515 and the ensuing Star Chamber case have already been mentioned.[8] The petition to the King which

---

[5] Brand II p154.

[6] Surtees Society vol 137 p94 (No 139) and p25 (No 24).

[7] AA 3rd series vol VII p96 (or Seldon Soc vol 25).

[8] Chapter 2.

initiated the case was made by the "Mayor, Aldermen and certain of the commoners" of Newcastle and the defendants were the "Artificers, Burgesses and Gild Merchants". The first paragraph of their answer to the petition is worth quoting here: "In times past said artificers bought and sold all manner of merchandise at their free liberty according to Royal grants confirmed by the King without any agreement with other crafts. The said customs were of greater profit to the King than now, as occurs by books of record and the town richer in goods and better governed. In the grants made upon the first corporation the liberty of buying and selling was given to all the Burgesses and Gild Merchants of the town". The reference to the first corporation of the town must refer to John's Charter of 1216 which had been confirmed by every succesive sovereign. The Burgesses' complaints and the subsequent proceedings bear a striking resemblance to those of 1305. The Burgesses were, as before, fighting for their liberty to trade freely without the restrictions which the merchants were trying to put on their rights. The 1515 proceedings also follow the pattern of the disputes in 1342 and 1438 but, although the burgess artificers called themselves the Gild Merchants and had every justification for doing so, it would seem that there was in fact no operative Gild Merchant distinct from the Common Gild still in existence. The old Gild Merchant, though not forgotten, having been submerged in the common gild some time before the middle of the fifteenth century, had virtually ceased to have even a theoretical existence, perhaps as a result of Henry IV's Charter of 1400. The common gild was the governing body of the town and itself was under the control, not directly of the Burgesses in Gild, but of the Mayor, Sheriff, Aldermen and officials elected annually by the Burgesses, as specified in 1342. This situation had given rise to the Burgesses' complaint that the Mayor and Aldermen, sitting in the King's Court, had refused to do justice to their suit.

We may well say that by this time (1515) the Gild Merchant existed only in legal theory, if at all. In the words of Gross: "Its Aldermen and other peculiar officers, its whole organisation as a distinctive entity had vanished. It had merged its identity in that of the general municipal organism."

Mention should be made here of a licence granted by Henry VII in 1506[9] to the "Governors of the Gild Merchant of Newcastle", empowering them to buy wool and wool fells of the growth of Northumberland, Cumberland, Westmorland, Durham, Allerton and Richmond, and to ship them to foreign parts. This licence used the expression "Governors of the Gild Merchant", but also uses the expression "Governors and whole Community of the Gild of Merchants" and it is clear that the latter is more correct. The licence was to the members of the fellowship of Merchants and the same licence is included in the Charter of incorporation subsequently granted to fifteen members of the fellowship of Merchants by Edward VI on 1st September 1547.

The Gild Merchant granted by King John to the Burgesses was still operative as late as 1515 though its functions had been taken over by the Common Gild (possibly as a result of the re organisation by Henry IV's charter of 1400). The evidence of the Merchants in the 1515 case referred to the trouble between the Burgesses in 1438 and this shows the continuity. The craftsmen in the 1515 enquiry called themselves "Gild Merchants" and the evidence given by them demonstrates that they were carrying on their daily business notwithstanding the efforts of the Merchants to prevent them. It is clear that they had not forgotten their rights under the old Gild Merchant. The decision of the Court of Star Chamber in granting some limited rights to the craftsmen by implication recognised the existence of the older ancient rights.

The position as settled by the Star Chamber decree was affected by the later formation of the common council, followed again by re organisation of the political system of the town government leading on to the Charters of Queen Elizabeth. Looking at the Gild Merchant aspect of the matter, it may be that at this stage we finde the origins of the dual control presently operated by the Newcastle upon Tyne Town Moor Act 1988.

It has sometimes been claimed that the Merchant Adventurers' Company, chartered by Edward VI in 1547, was

---

[9] Gross II p185, also Brand II p225.

the same body as, or at least the successor of, the former Gild Merchant, but these claims do not appear to have been made by the Merchant Adventurers' Company. In 1305 the rich Burgesses had claimed to be a Gild Merchant by ancient custom, but did not claim under King John's Charter of 1216, the benefit of which was claimed in general terms by the poor Burgesses. The Exchequer Court on that occasion ruled against the claim of the rich Burgesses to have special privileges which other Burgesses did not have. The meeting of the Mayor and Burgesses in 1342 is described as the "Full Gild" which must mean the governing body of the town, rather than the Gild Merchant, as its business was nearly all connected with matters of town government. The same observation applies to the common gild in 1438, the decision of which is clearly an act of town government rather than a matter of trade regulation only. The Court of Star Chamber in 1515 made an administrative order which placed the Merchant companies (the Drapers, Boothmen and Mercers) in a special position, but the only reference to the Gild Merchant in those proceedings appears to be the description of the artificers, Burgesses and Gild Merchants, also referred to in another document as the artificers, commoners and Gild Merchants. From this it would seem that the Drapers, Mercers and Boothmen's companies were not claiming to be the old Gild Merchant. The fellowship of Merchants did claim in 1644 that they had been "an ancient company of merchants ever since King John's time" and had been confirmed by several grants confirmed by Royal Charters, referring no doubt to the wool licences and Edward VI's Charter of 1547 confirmed by Queen Mary, Queen Elizabeth and King James I. The fellowship also claimed that "the merchants in Newcastle are an ancient Gild of merchants ever since the seventeenth year of King John,"[10] which suggests that they were now claiming to be the same body as the Gild Merchant referred to in King John's Charter. The sixteenth century minutes of the Merchant company, however, repeatedly refer to the company as a fellowship and

---

[10] Surtees Society vol 101 (1899) pp116, 117.

this practice continued as late as the early eighteenth century, though the name company was increasingly used from the commonwealth period onwards. It seems therefore that the Merchant Adventurers' company itself did not seriously claim to be identical with the Gild Merchant.

The persons who were incorporated by the Charter of Edward VI were fifteen members of the "fellowship of Merchants" who were also members of the "fellowship of Merchant Adventurers in the parts of Brabant", together with all other of those merchants inhabiting the town and county of Newcastle upon Tyne. They were incorporated to be the "fellowship of Merchant Adventurers in Newcastle upon Tyne" by the name of the Governor, Assistants, Wardens and Fellowship of Merchant Adventurers inhabiting within the town and county of Newcastle upon Tyne. This Charter of Incorporation which does not mention any Gild Merchant contains detailed regulations of the conduct of the new Company with various powers, including power to admit new members and power to buy and ship wools and wool fells in much the same terms as were set out in the earlier licences. It appears that this new Company was intended to be affiliated to the London (or National) Company of the Merchant Adventurers to which certain dues were payable, the amount of which was agreed at £8 per annum. These dues and the affiliation to the London Company caused a very long dispute.[11]

Gross comments that the contrast between the Company of Merchant Adventurers on the one hand and the old Gild Merchant on the other is striking. The Merchant Adventurers' Company had to do wholly with foreign trade and its members were forbidden to exercise a manual occupation or even to be retail shopkeepers. The Gild Merchant, however, consisted mainly of small shopkeepers and artisans. He remarks that there appear to be three stages in the history of the word Merchant. First it embraced all who in their trades were in any way concerned with buying and selling, including petty shopkeepers and small handicraftsmen. During the fifteenth

---

[11] For details see Surtees Society vol 101 (1899).

and greater part of the sixteenth century it applied pre-
eminently to all who made a business of buying for resale –
retailers as well as wholesalers – but manual craftsmen not
being included. It then came to have its present meaning of an
extensive dealer. In conception the old Gild Merchant
represents the first stage, the Companies or Fellowships of
Merchants the second, and the Staplers and Merchant
Adventurers the third. The Merchant Adventurers' Company
of Newcastle upon Tyne consisted primarily of three trade or
merchant companies, which continued to exist after the
Merchant Adventurers' Company was formed. These
companies, or mysteries (i.e. misteries = trades) as they were
termed, functioned in the electoral system of the town and
continued their separate existence until a new electoral system
was set up in 1836, since when those three companies have lost
their separate identities, being absorbed into the Merchant
Adventurers' Company. It seems, therefore, that any modern
claims that the Merchant Adventurers' Company is the same
body as the Gild Merchant created or confirmed by King
John's Charter cannot be supported. As Gross remarked, the
Gild Merchant was the predecessor not the progenitor of the
later Merchants Company, but having drawn this distinction, it
must also be admitted that the Merchant Adventurers'
Company of Newcastle upon Tyne is of very respectable
antiquity, having been incorporated and confirmed by several
Royal Charters and having a distinguished history in the trade
and commerce (as well as the local government) of Newcastle
for more than four centuries, and having roots going back to
the twelfth century.

CHAPTER 4

The Court of Guild

The Court of Guild (the governing body of the Freemen) is probably the most ancient institution still existing in Newcastle, although since the Municipal Corporations Act 1835 it has lost most of its powers, retaining only those which relate to the organisation of the Freemen and the management of their affairs.[1]

In Anglo Saxon England, and indeed for long after, the government of the towns or boroughs consisted basically of the Folk Moot, a meeting of the free inhabitants of the community concerned, later known as the borough court. Many of the boroughs became possessions of the King or regional Earl. They were headed by an official in some cases elected by the community or in other cases imposed by the King or Earl. This official was known in some boroughs as Provost,[2] in others as Prefect, Reeve or Bailiff. Provost and Prefect were virtually the same by different names but the difference may well be that the Provost was elected whilst the Prefect was imposed by Royal authority. In Newcastle the official was the Provost and the customs of the town in the reign of Henry I throw some light on his responsibilities and powers. The Provost became known in the thirteenth century as the Mayor. King Edgar in the ninth century had ordered that the Borough Court should be held three times in each year. David of Scotland, when occupying Newcastle about the mid-twelfth century, included in his Laws of the Four Boroughs, the first of which were copied directly from the customs of Newcastle, a law that the three meetings should be at Michaelmas, Christmas and Easter. The elections of the Provost were to take place at Michaelmas. It is therefore probable that these were the meeting times observed in Newcastle in the twelfth century and earlier. Documentary evidence shows that the dates still observed for these meetings, namely the second Monday after Michaelmas Day, the second

---

[1] Now confirmed by the Town Moor Act 1988 s16.

[2] The origins of Newcastle, R F Walker p13 n37.

Monday after (the end of) the Feast of Christmas and the second Monday after Easter Day, were days when meetings of the Borough Court were held in the twelfth century. These meetings were referred to as Courts or Full Courts. The alternative name of Full Guild came into use in the fourteenth century, but the days of meeting remained the same, as they still do, thus showing the continuity. It would seem that the reason for the change of style was that the Borough Court and the Court of the Merchant Guild had in effect been amalgamated so far as government of the town was concerned, and were referred to as "the Guild", as indeed it still is.

Newcastle was formally incorporated by Queen Elizabeth in 1589 by the name of the Mayor and Burgesses of Newcastle upon Tyne and the Charter of incorporation provided that the Mayor and Burgesses assembled together should have various powers of town government in parallel with a Common Council consisting of the Mayor, Sheriff and Aldermen, together with twenty-four Burgesses elected by the twelve leading companies of Freemen. The powers of the Mayor and Burgesses included a power to regulate the merchants and craftsmen and their affairs. James I granted another Charter, virtually the same in this respect as Queen Elizabeth's, but inserted a clause under which the acts made or agreed by the Mayor and Burgesses assembled "in Guild" were not to be effective in relation to the property of the town, nor was the Common Seal to be used, unless agreed by the Common Council. This was a severe curtailment of the powers of the Mayor and Burgesses, though they continued on occasions to exercise their powers in town government. The name "Court of Guild" seems to have come into use in the last quarter of the eighteenth century, probably to emphasise the Guild's standing as part of the legal government of the town at a time when the Common Council were denying even its limited authority as granted by the governing Charters.

The Muncipal Corporations Act 1835 abolished the Common Council and destroyed the local government powers of the Mayor and Burgesses, new powers being vested in the New Town Council. The Act, however, did not affect the powers of the Guild in relation to Freemen's affairs in so far as such powers were not inconsistent with the Act. To what extent these powers continued in existence is an interesting subject for discussion, but is now academic as the Town Moor Act 1988 (Section 16) gives power to the Court of Guild to regulate the Freemen's affairs.

This section provides that "the Court of Guild shall be held as heretofore consisting of the Close Guild at which the Companies of Freemen shall be represented by the Stewards and Wardens thereof and the Open Guild at which the Lord Mayor of the City or his Deputy shall preside and all Freemen shall be entitled to attend". The Open Guild is clearly the traditional meeting of "the Mayor and Burgesses in Guild assembled". The Close Guild, which came into existence at the end of the eighteenth century, requires a separate explanation.

In order to trace the origins of the Close Guild it is necessary to go back to the sixteenth century. In 1557, perhaps earlier, a Common Council consisting of the twenty-four electors as assistants had been set up by the Council of the North, apparently as a reorganisation of the town's government.[3] This Common Council was fully organised in 1561, made up of the Mayor, ten Aldermen, the Sheriff, and twenty-four electors. The Charter of Elizabeth in 1589 formally incorporated the Burgesses for the first time, and confirms both the Guild and the Common Council as bodies to rule the town's affairs. The reason for this somewhat curious arrangement was no doubt that the three full Guild meetings were too far apart to deal satisfactorily with matters that arose between times, the Common Council being seen as a sub-committee of the Guild or perhaps the Guild as a check on the activities of the Common Council. Elizabeth's Charter of 1600 continued the arrangement but James I's Charter of 1604 was clearly intended to put the Common Council into a controlling position without destroying the Guild. The end result of all the excitements of the seventeenth century was that these two Charters were considered to be the governing Charters of the town and the Common Council effectively took

[3] See Brand II pp. 181, 182.

charge of the town government, although the Guild continued to meet regularly but had a decreasing share of the administration.

Thus the Common Council became known as (or called itself) the "governing part of the Corporation". This led in time to the Common Council's attitude that the Guild had no powers or part in the government of the town and was no more than an ancient formality. The Freemen, and particularly the Stewards of the Companies, had always attended the Guild meetings, considering them to be the forum for matters relating to the management of the town's affairs. The attitude of the Common Council caused great dissatisfaction to the Freemen and led to meetings of the Stewards of the Companies, who were recognised as a body by the Town Moor Act 1774. The events leading up to this Act and the results over the next century are described in greater detail in Chapter VIII. The Stewards' organisation was set up in the last decades of the eighteenth century and before 1800 they had a Chairman, Secretary and Treasurer and were meeting regularly. These meetings, then known as the Body of the Stewards, in or before 1808 started to elect a committee, named the Herbage Committee, to look after the management of the Town Moor and the interests of the resident Freemen and widows. The Stewards did not use the Guildhall for their meetings but in time a practice arose whereby the Stewards assembled in the Guildhall to discuss the Freemen's business before the proclamation of the full or Open Guild. This prior meeting of the Stewards, which of course was private, became known as the "Close" (meaning private) Guild.

In the course of the next half century, the Herbage Committee developed into a committee dealing with Freemen's affairs generally, and was usually styled the Stewards Committee. This was recognised by the Newcastle upon Tyne Improvement Act 1870, which authorised the Stewards Committee to act for and on behalf of resident Freemen and widows for all purposes connected with the Town Moor, and gave the Committee other powers, including that of making bye-laws which were duly made and approved. These powers, varied in detail but without any very substantial change, were re-enacted in the Town Moor Act 1988.

Under this Act, the corporate guild now consists of the Close Guild and the Open Guild. The Close Guild is a meeting of the Stewards and Wardens of the Companies, who elect the Stewards Committee and transact the ordinary business of the Freemen, including a review of the activities of the Stewards Committee. After the Close Guild is finished or adjourned the Open Guild is proclaimed under the presidency of the Lord Mayor. All Freemen are entitled to attend this meeting. Any Freeman having any grievance relating to public affairs in the City is entitled by tradition to address the Lord Mayor, though in practice any such grievances are dealt with through the Close Guild and included if necessary in the address to the Lord Mayor by the Chairman of the Freemen.

It will be seen that the Open Guild is the traditional meeting of the Lord Mayor and Burgesses (Freemen) in Guild assembled, whilst the Close Guild is a meeting of the Company stewards representing their members, with the Stewards' Committee acting in the role of an elected cabinet.

The Open Guild is attended by the Lord Mayor or his deputy who presides. With him are the Mace and Sword Bearers, the Town Clerk (now known as Head of Administration) and the Registration Officer. The court is then proclaimed by the Mace Bearer in the following terms: "All persons having anything to do at a Court of Guild held here this day before the Right Worshipful Lord Mayor, let them come forward, and they shall be heard. All non-Freemen are strictly charged and commanded to depart this court immediately under penalty of £5 or pain of imprisonment. God save the Queen". It is perhaps needless to remark that the form of proclamation is archaic and the court no longer has power to enforce payment of £5 or to imprison non-Freemen. The Chairman of the Freemen then addresses the Lord Mayor and Town Clerk, referring as necessary to any matters of interest or concern, and they reply to the matters raised. The registration officer then calls over a list of applicants for the freedom (this process is known as calling the applicant's guilds) and any business requiring confirmation by the Open Guild can then be put to the vote. After this business is concluded the Mace Bearer proclaims: "All persons may now depart and give their attendance at the next Court of Guild. God Save the Queen". It is the usual practice for the Vice-Chairman of the Freemen to call for three cheers for the Lord Mayor and the Town Clerk, and the Town Clerk calls for three cheers for the Chairman of the Freemen.

The organisation of the Freemen, reflecting growth and adaptation over centuries, is somewhat complex and may be considered illogical and capable of improvement. In practice, however, it seems to work quite effectively and with sufficient flexibility to enable further amendments to be made, if and when required.

CHAPTER 5

The Freemen's Companies

How and when the Freemen's Companies originated in the town is not known. Twelve of the companies are enumerated in the Articles of Government agreed and adopted at a full Guild in February 1342 and subsequently confirmed by Charter of Edward III.[1] The twelve named companies are styled misteries, and described as the most honourable decent and honest of the town, which must imply that there were others, but this does not indicate how long the companies may have been in existence. In general terms it may be said that the basic form of such organisations was imported from the continent after the Norman Conquest, though the English companies had no direct connection with similar organisations in France. In the twelfth and thirteenth centuries such companies proliferated in nearly all the principal towns.

No individual companies are referred to in the record of the 1305 Exchequer Court case except that the rich Burgesses claimed to be a Gild Merchant. When questioned as to their authority for this claim they were unable to produce any, other than alleged ancient custom. This may have had some basis in fact but it is noticeable that they did not claim to be the Gild Merchant established or confirmed by King John's Charter in 1216.[2] Brand refers to a document stating that in the eighth year of Edward III (1334) the King, being in person at Newcastle, established the Mayor with authority and confirmed the election of magistrates, merchants, Freemen and the community of that place. It does not seem very probable that this reorganisation of the then local government included the setting up of individual companies, though it does suggest that the merchants' ancient company may have been approved. It should be mentioned that companies have been known at different periods by different names, e.g. company, mistery, fellowship, gild or fraternity, all however referring to the same

---

[1] Brand II p157.

[2] Appendix 3.

type of association. None of them could claim to be legally incorporated unless they had been set up by or obtained the grant of a Royal Charter.

The twelve misteries referred to in 1342 were the Drapers (wool merchants), Mercers, Skinners, Taylors, Saddlers, Boothmen (corn merchants), Bakers, Tanners, Cordwainers, Butchers, Smiths and Fullers. It should be noted that the Fellowship of Merchants in the sixteenth century claimed to be made up of the wool merchants, mercers and corn merchants. These three misteries retained their separate identities until the Municipal Corporations Reform Act 1835, after which they were gradually absorbed by the present Merchant Adventurers' Company, and no longer exist as separate Companies.

The twelve misteries throughout the Middle Ages and later were generally recognised as more important than the other companies, perhaps because they had an essential function in the annual elections of the Mayor and civic officials. James I by a charter of 31st March 1604 brought fifteen other companies (styled bye trades) into the initial stages of the elections, though this would seem to have been a formality rather than an effective innovation. The fifteen bye trades were: the Masters and Mariners, Weavers, Barber-Surgeons with Chandlers, Cutlers, Shipwrights, Coopers, House Carpenters, Masons, Glovers (later amalgamated with the Skinners), Joiners (separated from the House Carpenters in 1589), Millers, Curriers, Felt Makers and Armourers, Colliers, Paviors and Carriagemen, Slaters, Plumbers, Glaziers, Pewterers and Painters (this company included Goldsmiths, but they are not mentioned).

There are also some companies still in existence which were not included in the fifteen bye trades, namely:

1 The Goldsmiths, who from 1536 had been part of the fifteenth bye trade, were separated from the Plumbers, Glaziers, Pewterers and Painters in 1717 after a new statutory Goldsmiths company was set up by Act of Parliament in 1703. The Goldsmiths finally separated from the Plumbers company in 1717.

2 The Scriveners. This company set up in 1675 had a somewhat chequered career. Being reconstituted in 1828 and again in 1974 by an Act of the Corporation of Newcastle upon Tyne in exercise of its chartered powers a few days before the old Corporation itself ceased to exist by virtue of the Local Government Act 1972.

3 The Wallers, Bricklayers and Plasterers.

4 The Ropemakers.

5 The Upholsterers, Tinplate Workers and Stationers.

Brand also lists some extinct companies namely the Waits or Musicians, the Mettors, the Porters, the Cooks, the Spicers, the Furbishers, the Swordslippers, the Bowyers, the Fletchers, the Spurriers, the Girdlers, the Vintners and the Keelmen. The Watermen or Ferrymen were apparently an organised body before 1656 when they petitioned the Corporation to be made an incorporated company, which request was renewed in 1675 and 1698, but no action appears to have been taken on this petition.

The Freemen's companies are collectively referred to as incorporated companies. This expression has been in use since at least as early as the middle years of the eighteenth century and perhaps a century before that. The word incorporated does not imply legal incorporation, for the law has been since the early Middle Ages that only the Crown could set up a legally incorporated body, though the corporate body of a town could make a fraternity. The Mayor and Burgesses (i.e. the Court of Guild) of Newcastle claimed to be a corporation by prescription and also claimed a right to set up the Freemen's companies by means of a legal document authorising the formation of the company and laying down the regulations for its perpetual succession and granting it various powers. These documents are commonly referred to as Company Charters, thereby giving rise to the misunderstanding that companies were formed by Royal Charter (as was the practice with the livery companies in London). Similarly the execution of the document by the Mayor, Sheriff and Aldermen on behalf of the Guild came to be known as incorporation.

There are three bodies of Freemen commonly known as companies which are different from the other companies in that they have been founded or confirmed by express Royal Charters. These are Trinity House, the Merchant Adventurers and the Fraternity of Hostmen.

Trinity House was originally a religious foundation whose mission was to rescue and support distressed and aged seamen. It is reputed (though this may be a mistake of identity) to have been set up at its origin in Berwick-upon-Tweed but violently expelled from that town and removed to Newcastle. In January 1492[3] the company purchased the site of the present House in Broad Chare. Brand states that they were a corporate body at this time but apparently not legally incorporated as the purchase was effected through trustees. In 1536 Henry VIII granted a Charter of Incorporation to encourage the art of navigation and authorising the fraternity or gild to make laws for the maintenance of the Port of Tyne, in particular to erect two towers at North Shields (now known as the Low and High Lights) and to deal with the pilotage of the river and Port of Tyne.[4] The jurisdiction of Trinity House, then or later, extended not only to the River Tyne but also to the north-east coast between Whitby and Holy Island. The precise relationship between Trinity House and the company of Masters and Mariners is difficult to see clearly. For many purposes the House and the company are treated as one but this is not exactly accurate. The freedom of the town gained by apprenticeship to a free brother of Trinity House descends to the sons of such a free brother, but the freedom of Trinity House itself does not, unless such a son becomes a sailor for seven years. The only advantage which free mariners' sons in this respect have is that they need not be indentured as apprentices, it being sufficient if they are sailors for seven years whether bound or not. It is noticeable that in some accounts of the companies the bye trade is denominated Mariners company and the combined name Masters and Mariners may

---

[3] This date should perhaps be 1502.

[4] Further Royal Charters were granted by Elizabeth, James I, Charles II and James II.

signify that the mariners were the brethren of the mariners company whereas the masters were members of Trinity House. In the 1833 Parliamentary Commission investigation into the Corporation and its affairs Mr Thomas Gibson, Secretary of Trinity House, gave evidence that the younger brethren generally comprised every person free of the house not an elder brother, the number of younger brethren being indefinite. This appears to be an extension of the Charter which prescribed twelve elder and ten younger brethren. It would seem from all this that there are strictly speaking two bodies concerned, namely the legal Corporation of Trinity House and the unincorporated Masters and Mariners Company, but the division between these two bodies is so blurred that they are commonly treated as one.

The second company having curious anomalies in its history and constitution is the Merchant Adventurers. The rich Burgesses in 1305 claimed to be a merchant gild but not the Gild Merchant of the town created or confirmed by King John in 1216. They produced no authority for their alleged gild and the judgement of the Exchequer Court was against their claim. In the 1342 Articles for government of the town no Gild Merchant or company of merchants is mentioned although the three merchant companies, the Drapers (wool merchants), Mercers and Boothmen (corn merchants) were named amongst the twelve most important companies. There can be no doubt that the merchants became a substantial and influential group before 1480, when they had their own organisation and meeting hall. Towards the end of the fifteenth century there emerged a body describing itself as the "Fellowship of Merchants".[5] This would seem to have been a body distinct from the Gild Merchant, which comprised all Burgesses. The Fellowship of Merchants is not mentioned in the Star Chamber proceedings of 1515 although the Drapers (wool merchants), Mercers and Boothmen (corn merchants) are mentioned, there are repeated references to foreign as well

---

[5] It is possible that the merchants were organised as a group much earlier, even as early as Henry II's charter in 1175 (AA3 3rd series XII p260), but if so the absence of records or references is remarkable.

as local trade. Indeed, looking at the Star Chamber proceedings as a whole, it is clear that the dispute was between the members of the fellowship of merchants on the one side and the remaining craft companies claiming to have liberty to trade as members of the old Gild Merchant on the other side. Both sides were partly satisfied by the resulting decree.

Edward VI, by a charter dated 1st September 1547, incorporated the governor, twelve assistants, two wardens, fifteen named merchants and all those other merchants inhabiting the town and county of Newcastle who were members of the fellowship of Merchant Venturers in Brabant beyond the seas, as a fellowship of Merchant Venturers within the town to be one body incorporated of themselves for ever. The official name was The Governor, Assistants, Wardens and Fellowship of Merchant Venturers inhabiting the Town and County of Newcastle upon Tyne. Amongst numerous other provisions the newly incorporated fellowship was authorised to admit any of the King's subjects dwelling in Newcastle. This charter was ratified and confirmed by Queen Mary and Queen Elizabeth. The charter does not expressly restrict admission to the members of the merchant companies, though this can be inferred from the fact that only members of the merchant companies could carry on the various merchant trades. It is noticeable that the incorporated body called itself a Fellowship until the early years of James I, after which the name company came into use as an alternative. The expression "Fellowship" seems to have died out about the time of the Restoration. The company did in 1644 claim to have been an ancient Company of Merchants since King John's time, which looks like a claim to identify themselves with the Gild Merchant referred to in King John's Charter of 1216. This seems to be the only occasion on which such a claim was actually made and is inconsistent with the position taken up by the merchants in the Star Chamber proceedings of 1515. Whatever the antecedents of the Fellowship of Merchants may have been, the Merchant Adventurers Company is quite clearly the creation not of King John but of Edward VI. It is now regarded as similar (except for its Royal Charter) to the other Freemen's Companies.

The third company which is unusually different from the others is the Fraternity of Hostmen commonly called the Hostmen's Company. In the Middle Ages the practice of hosting foreign merchants by local ones was widespread and indeed regulated by Acts of Parliament. Hosts were to be assigned by the town authority and were responsible for the good behaviour of the visiting merchant who was also known as a host. Sometime before the Star Chamber case in 1515 a Company of Hostmen had been formed within the merchants company. John Robson, a taylor, gave evidence that he had occupied the craft of a Hostman and was compelled to agree with the Hostman craft company and paid a fine of six shillings and eightpence. Since that agreement he had been Steward of the craft and had sued various men for occupying it without agreement. The Hostmen's Company must therefore have been in existence for some time, probably a considerable time, before the evidence was taken. To this company was assigned the trade in coal, grindstones and whetstones. These trades were expanding rapidly in the sixteenth century. Coal had been a town rather than a private trade and a source of revenue from which the fee farm due to the Crown was paid. The Mayor and Bailiffs in 1362 petitioned the King to repeal a prohibition on the export of coal which they said was the only town trade.

Shortly after the Star Chamber case, it is clear from the books of the Merchants' Company that there was some overhaul of the relationship between the two companies, several members of the Hostmen's Company being charged with some form of adjustment, known as Hostmen's money. The coal trade being very lucrative, the Hostmen became a very powerful influence in town affairs. The Hostmen's Fraternity (Company) was more closely connected with the town administration than the other companies. Part of the admission fees was paid to the Town Chamberlains and the town paid for the Fraternity's Corpus Christi play. These items seem to suggest that the members of the Fraternity, perhaps even before the Fraternity was formed, were part of the town administration forming the department that dealt with the coal trade as a town trade, and this would also account for the fact that many, if not all members, were also members of the Merchants' Company.

Amongst the Hostmen's responsibilities was that of collecting the Royal tax of two pence per chaldron on coal exported. This tax fell very substantially into arrears, so much so that Queen Elizabeth or her advisers abandoned the arrears on the Hostmen's agreeing to pay a substituted tax of a shilling per chaldron, which as the coal trade expanded became immensely valuable. Charles II settled the tax upon his illegitimate son the Duke of Richmond and it became known as the Richmond shilling. The payment was made to the Duke or his Trustees until 1799 when the Treasury purchased it for an annual payment of £19,000, which was afterwards commuted for a capital sum of £633,333 6s 9d. On a petition from the Hostmen's Company, in view of the changed conditions of the coal trade, the tax was repealed and ceased to be payable in March 1831. The capital sum, or a large part of it, was expended by the Duke of Richmond on the purchase of the Goodwood Estates in Sussex where the famous Goodwood racecourse is situated.

The Fraternity of Hostmen was legally incorporated by clauses in the Great Charter of Queen Elizabeth in 1600. Forty-eight named persons were incorporated under the name of the Governor, Stewards and Brethren of the Fraternity of Hostmen of Newcastle upon Tyne. Most of the named members were also members of the Merchants Adventurers Company and nearly all appear in records as Mayor, Aldermen, Sheriff and Common Councillors. It seems clear that the Hostmen's Company, allied with the Merchant Adventurers, provided nearly all of the oligarchy who ruled the town until the town government was reformed in 1836.

One of the interesting features of the Hostmen's Company was that any burgess of the town was entitled to be admitted on making application and paying the admission fee, part of which, as mentioned above, went to the Town Chamberlains. This seems to reflect the old Gild Merchant. The right of admission to the company was disputed from the time of the

Charter and was confused by a further Charter from James I. The company itself did its best to remain an exclusive body and the full extent of the rights of admission was not finally settled until 1840.

The Hostmen's Company of Newcastle upon Tyne is thought to be the only company of Hostmen existing in the world. There was formerly a company of Hostmen at Yarmouth which dealt with the fish trade but it seems to have disappeared in the late eighteenth century.

Of the misteries mentioned above, four, namely the Drapers, the Mercers, the Corn Merchants and the Fullers have become extinct (though three were absorbed into the Merchant Adventurers). Of the bye trades one, namely the Cutlers, has disappeared while of the other companies all survive. This surely is a remarkable instance of the persistence of human organisation.

Another organisation of Freemen was set up in 1972 by the Court of Guild. This is known as the Gild of Freemen of Newcastle upon Tyne and all Freemen are urged on their admission to join it. The objects of this association are to preserve the freedom generally, to bring the Freemen of the City together and to promote social, cultural and educational facilities for Freemen and their families, including in particular meetings of those Freemen who take an interest in the history of the institution. Underlying its formation was the need to maintain links with those Freemen who, for whatever reason, have not been admitted to membership of any of the trade or craft companies and are not directly represented by any Stewards.

Some Freemen have greater rights than others. There is a dual freedom of Newcastle, namely the basic Freedom of the City and the freedom of one or more of the existing Freemen's Companies. Whatever the practice may have been in the later Middle Ages, it seems clear that after 1600 no-one could be admitted to the freedom of a company until first admitted to the freedom of the City, but some of those admitted to the freedom of the City do not in fact proceed to take up the freedom of a company. This might be because the individual concerned did not wish to pay the admission fee or to practise a craft in which he had been apprenticed, or indeed saw no advantage in becoming a member of a company. Thus arose a quite considerable class of Freemen ("non-Company keepers") who although free of the town are not members of any company, and have no direct voice in the management of Freemen's affairs.

The right of admission to a company operates on the same lines as the right of admission to the freedom of the town, i.e. a father who was not admitted to his company could not pass on a similar right to his sons (though a company could admit as a matter of grace and favour grandsons or remoter issue who have been admitted to the freedom of the City). Thus the Freemen can be divided into two categories, the company keepers and the non-company keepers. Companies are presently being asked to consider reviewing their rules, if any, in respect of the exclusion of "non-Company Keepers" by admitting Feemen to companies through which they hail. This, however, is a domestic matter for the companies concerned. Another division amongst the Freemen is that of residence within the City boundaries. The resident Freemen and resident widows of Freemen are entitled to the grazing rights on the Town Moor, but non-residents are not so entitled.

CHAPTER 6

The Admission of Freemen

The right of admission to the freedom of the city (or the freelage as it is termed in Newcastle) is a legal franchise enforceable at law by those entitled to it. Under the provisions of the Local Government Act 1972 Section 248(3) it is the duty of the Lord Mayor to admit those entitled and by implication to refuse admission to those not entitled. The right arises in two ways, by patrimony or by servitude.

Admission by Patrimony

One of the customs of Newcastle in the reign of Henry I was "if a burgess have a son he shall be in his father's freedom if he be with his father". The version of this custom which appears in the Laws of the Four Boroughs (which were formulated by David of Scotland when he was in occupation of Newcastle about the middle of the twelfth century) is slightly more explicit "the son of a burgess shall have the same liberty of buying and selling as his father has so long as he shall be at his father's table but when he departs from him he shall not enjoy that liberty unless he shall be a burgess."[1] This custom may be capable of more than one interpretation but its general purport is clear. It records as already existing the practice that the son of a burgess is entitled to become a burgess himself. This is still the custom in Newcastle: all the lawful sons of a freeman are entitled to admission. By a regulation of the Common Council made in 1654 in accordance with its chartered powers no-one may be admitted a freeman before attaining the age of twenty.[2] The preliminary formalities may be taken before but the actual ceremony of admission may not take place until after the young man's twentieth birthday. Adopted or illegitimate sons and aliens are not eligible for admission. There are no restrictions on the place of residence of the father or of the birth of the son. It is not unusual for sons of Freemen who have emigrated permanently or temporarily

[1] AA4 vol I p175.

[2] NRS vol I p178.

to other countries to travel great distances in order to be admitted to the freelage and provided they have retained their British nationality no difficulty arises. Complications arising out of the modern law relating to change of nationality can easily be envisaged but no difficulty on this score has as yet been experienced.

The custom of Newcastle has been that only sons and not grandsons of Freemen are eligible, though it is arguable that in law the term "son" may include "grandson". Sons born before the father takes up his freelage are admitted but the son of a father who, although entitled, does not take up his freelage is not admitted because the father was not a freeman. This sometimes causes great disappointment as the consequence of a father who is entitled to admission failing (whether intentionally or by inadvertence or even through circumstances outside his control) to be admitted is to debar his descendants. This rule sometimes appears to operate harshly and the question has been discussed in recent years whether it could be altered and if so how and to what extent, but no conclusions have been reached.

Admission by Servitude

The second method by which a person can become entitled to admission is servitude (otherwise apprenticeship) to a freeman. The system of apprenticeship came into being in England in the fourteenth century though like many English legal institutions it may well have existed for a long time before being recognised by the law. When the system was first recognised only the sons of men having substantial property could be apprenticed. The advantages of the system, however, were such that it was extended. It was regulated by a number of statutes in the fifteenth century, details of which are now unimportant except that the later statutes laid down that the minimum period of apprenticeship should be seven years. This continued to be the law until 1814 when, after much public discussion for and against, the minimum period was abolished by Act of Parliament.[3]

---

[3]   53 Geo 3 Chap 96. See also Surtees Society vol 93p v/vii.

In Newcastle the detailed regulations for apprenticeship were considered to be matters within the jurisdiction of the various companies of Freemen which controlled their own affairs. The period of the apprenticeship varied in different trades from time to time depending on the economic conditions and the consequent desire of the existing members to maintain, increase or decrease their numbers. (The same observation applies to the admission of Freemen generally and the policy of various towns with regard to their Freemen changed from time to time from restrictive to permissive and back again depending upon the economic conditions of trade and manufacture in the particular town concerned.) The practice at one time might therefore be substantially different from that at another time. Similarly and as part of the same economic process the companies made and altered regulations from time to time governing the number of apprentices any of their members might take.

Basically the rule for admission of apprentices was and is that all the apprentices of a freeman who have duly and faithfully served their time are entitled to be admitted Freemen themselves. This rule has, however, been subjected to a number of refinements, mostly of a restrictive nature and of doubtful validity. The customs of Newcastle with regard to apprentices being eligible for admission were in the period shortly prior to 1835 said to be: (1) that the master must be (a) a freeman or widow of a freeman carrying on his business (b) free of his company (c) carrying on the trade of his company (d) resident within the boundaries of the town during the whole period of apprenticeship; (2) that the Apprentice's indentures must have been enrolled by (a) the company and (b) the Town Clerk within a limited period; (3) that the apprentice must have served his time within the liberties of the town; (4) that the apprentice must be not less than twenty years of age at the date of admission; (5) that the period of apprenticeship must be a minimum of seven years. Most of these refinements were either illegal, disputed, inapplicable, variable or waived by the Corporation in some cases. It must be remembered that the Corporation of Newcastle i.e. the Mayor and Burgesses or the Common Council had chartered powers to make and change regulations for the Burgesses and their apprentices. It may well be that instead of making proper bye-laws in exercise of their chartered powers they preferred to deal with any individual cases of difficulty on an ad hoc basis. It was accepted though not expressly declared (probably being ancient custom) that the Master must be a freeman or the widow of a freeman carrying on his business. The only declared regulation by the Common Council (6 December 1654) was the twenty year age limit. Apprentices had certainly been made free whose masters were not members of the company of the trade concerned, if indeed there was any such company. The requirement that the apprentice must serve his time within the liberties of the town did not apply to apprentices of Merchants, Mariners or Shipwrights and the requirement of residence in town was sometimes flexible. The time limits for enrolment of indentures by the company and the Town Clerk were also flexible. The minimum period of seven years' apprenticeship was then the general law of the land but the requirement was, already as mentioned, abolished in 1814. There was therefore no legal minimum period after that time.

The Municipal Corporations Act 1835 which had such a drastic effect on the Freemen's rights and position preserves them only to applicants for admission who fulfilled (so far as were capable of being fulfilled according to the Act) every condition which would at the date of the Act have been a condition precedent to admission. The meaning of this requirement does not seem to have been elucidated by any legal decision. Bearing in mind that the Act was a general one applicable to a large number of boroughs with differing customs or chartered rights and differing rules as to the evidence necessary to establish a right to admission, we may well think that the conditions referred to are those conditions which are fundamental to a right of entitlement to admission and that compliance with local customs or requirements relating only to evidence, procedure or methods of admission is not a condition precedent for this purpose. The Act expressly prohibited admission by purchase or gift but left open other local means such as ownership of a burgage. In these cases the fact of lawful birth, marriage, apprenticeship, etc., would be a condition precedent but a practice as to the evidence normally or even invariably required to prove such fact would not be such a condition because the fact could be proved otherwise. It is possible that the Act contemplated such matters as local customs covering nationality, age, birth or residence within certain boundaries being conditions precedent to admission but this is not stated nor is it a necessary implication of the Act. The intention may have been only to ensure that no new methods of entitlement were invented rather than to restrict existing methods except gift or purchase. In any case certainty of the details of any condition alleged would be essential and would have to be proved, as compliance with an illegal, uncertain or variable practice could clearly not be a condition precedent to the acquisition of rights which were then of considerable value.

Like admission by patrimony, admission by servitude is of interest in modern times. Although apprenticeship still exists in some trades it has died out in many others, systems of vocational training being substituted. The Local Government Act 1972 refers to the admission of persons who are "associated with Freemen by way of employment" and these words were inserted in the Act as a deliberate substitution for the expression "servitude". Whether this has effected any change in the law may no doubt be a matter for discussion in years to come.

Admission by Purchase or Gift

The Municipal Corporations Act 1835 prohibited admission by purchase or gift. Admission by purchase is said never to have been known in Newcastle. The freedom was occasionally conferred by gift but was then usually restricted to being what was called "personal freedom only", i.e. it did not pass on to sons or apprentices.

Honorary Admission

Since 1835 the freedom of the town or city has been conferred on a number of distinguised persons, local regiments and some organisations but this has in all cases been an honorary freedom only which carries with it non of the rights, privileges or duties of the Freemen admitted to the roll.

The Formalities of Admission

As a first step to secure admission the applicant must have his name called at the Court of Guild, in the case of an applicant by patrimony once only but in the case of an apprentice three times. It has been customary for the name of the apprentice to be called three times at three successive Guilds at or about the conclusion of his period of service. It has, however, been said that the original object of this triple call was that the first should be at the commencement of the period of servitude in order to let the Freemen know who was being apprenticed, the second should be immediately prior to the conclusion of the period and the third at any time after the conclusion of the apprenticeship but before admission. This last call would be on the same basis as the applicant by patrimony namely to let the Freemen know who was about to be admitted so that in case of any irregularity objection could be made and the matter investigated. The method of making objection is for the objector, who may be any Freeman personally present at the Court of Guild, to say when the name is called 'I stop that guild'. The Town Clerk (now Head of Administration) or the official carrying out the duties of town clerk then notes 'stopped' against the name and the claim is referred to the Lord Mayor for examination and decision. His decision is a judicial one and can, if the circumstances warrant, be amended by legal process. The Lord Mayor is now responsible for establishing that the apprentice has duly complied with the current requirements, which themselves can be regulated by the Court of Guild except in so far as they may relate solely to the domestic affairs of any Company of Freemen.

In order to have his guild called the applicant should apply to the Stewards of the Company through which his father or master hails and the Stewards, having satisfied themselves as to the validity of the claim, then pass the application on to the Town Clerk or his officer to be called at the next Court of

Guild. This system ensures that the Stewards of the Company will be aware of the application and thus avoid the necessity of stopping the guild. In fact such stops are now very rare, the most recent having occurred some forty years ago when after enquiry it was found that the applicant claiming as the apprentice of a hostman many years before was in fact properly entitled. In practice this procedure is sometimes shortened by the applicant (who may not know who are the Stewards of his Company) applying directly to the Registrar at the Civic Centre who will inform the Stewards. An applicant, if in doubt, can seek guidance from the office of the Stewards' Committee of the Freemen, Moor Bank Lodge, Claremont Road.

After the guild has been called and the stop, if any, taken off, the applicant makes an appointment with the Lord Mayor to be sworn in and the ceremony of admission can then take place in the presence of the Lord Mayor or his deputy. The Town Clerk administers the traditional Freemen's Oath, now converted into a Declaration, and the new Freeman is then formally welcomed by the Lord Mayor. Whilst taking the Oath he holds an antique firearm, believed by civic officials to be a musket but which is in fact a blunderbuss, thus symbolising the words on the printed form of Declaration "Mr_____ is this day admitted a Freeman of the City of Newcastle upon Tyne and stands charged with a musket for the defence of the same". His name is then entered on the Roll of Freemen. It is customary for each newly admitted Freeman to present the Lord Mayor with an antique silver coin. The origin of this custom is not certain but it is of very long standing. Probably it reflects the mediaeval custom of giving an old coin as a token of gratitude: it does not seem to represent in any way a financial service to the recipient.

Freeman's Oath

The formal making of a Declaration (formerly an Oath) is the major part of the ceremony of admission of a Freeman. The formal Declaration is contained in the form of a Certificate of Admission which is signed by the appropriate official and the Lord Mayor. This is still known as the Oath Paper. In the eighteenth and ninetenth centuries the presence of the Mayor was not considered necessary and the Oath could be taken before any of the Magistrates of the town, i.e. the Mayor, Sheriff and Aldermen.

The form of Declaration now in use is as follows:

> "You declare that you shall from henceforth hold with our Sovereign Lady the Queen's Majesty that now is and with her heirs and successors Kings and Queens of Great Britain against all persons to live and to die: and maintain the peace and all the franchises of the City of Newcastle upon Tyne and be obedient to the Mayor Aldermen Sheriff and all other the officers of the same and their counsel keep: and no mans goods avow for yours unless he be as free as yourself and of the same franchise: and you shall observe and keep to the best of your power all lawful ordinances made by the common consent on High Court days: and all other things you shall do that belong to a Freeman of the said City"

The form then continues thus:

> "John Smith son of John Smith Tanner was this 30th day of June in the Year of Our Lord 1995 admitted a free burgess of this Corporation before the Right Worshipful Robert C. Brown Esq. Lord Mayor and stands charged with a musket for the defence thereof"

> Signed R. C. Brown Lord Mayor
> H. Warne Head of Administration

This form, somewhat elaborately printed on special paper, is then handed to the new Freeman to be retained by him as a certificate of his admission.

It will be noted that this so called oath is now a declaration rather than an oath, this no doubt being a consequence of the Statutory Declarations Act 1835 but the wording is identical with that given in Clark's Newcastle Remembrancer 1817, except that it then commenced with the words "You Swear" instead of "You Declare" and ended "So Help You God". When this form of oath was adopted is unknown but it would seem to be after the Great Charter of 42nd Elizabeth (1600) and probably after the restoration of Charles II for it is difficult to imagine an oath of this character being administered during the Commonwealth period.

The first part of the oath is clearly an Oath of Allegiance or Fealty to the Sovereign being followed by an obligation to maintain the King's peace. These items suggest that the origin of the oath may be connected with the oath of Arms which was required by Henry II's Assize of Arms 1181. Henry III in 1252 ordered the keeping of Watch and Ward and the maintenance of the Assize of Arms by the Burgesses of Boroughs, who were sworn to arms. The same system was carried on by later Sovereigns as a method of maintaining the King's peace. It seems, therefore, quite logical that the Freemen's admission Oath should include the obligation to be true to the Sovereign and to maintain his peace. There is, however, another possible origin for this part of the oath, namely that when Newcastle was part of the Royal Demesne each burgess on his admission to a burgage in the Borough Court would be called upon to swear fealty to the King as his feudal superior. Similarly when a non-Freeman was admitted to the freelage in accordance with the customs of Newcastle he would equally be required to swear fealty to the King as Lord of the Borough. These two possible origins are in fact virtually the same and go back at least to the early years of the twelfth century.

The next part of the oath, to maintain the franchises of the City and to be obedient to the Mayor, Aldermen, Sheriff and other officers of the same, is an obvious requirement from anyone being admitted to the privileges of the City. In its present form it could not go back earlier than 1400 when the Sheriff and Aldermen were first appointed. An oath in some such form as this would, however, be used in respect of admission to the Gild Merchant of Newcastle established or confirmed by King John in 1216, if indeed there ever was a separate Gild Merchant distinct from the Burgesses as a whole. There is no very clear distinction between the Government of the town and the Gild Merchant even when it disappeared from view and a new system of local government was instituted in or perhaps shortly before 1342. This part of the Freemen's oath could well apply to either aspect and again these two possible origins are virtually the same, going back to the end of the twelfth century or the early years of the thirteenth.

The next section of the oath "and no mans goods avow for yours" does not, as one might think in these days, mean making a false claim to someone else's property: it refers instead to the practice known as "colouring" a non-Freeman's goods. The object of this practice was to enable a non-Freeman to obtain the trading advantages and freedom from toll of a Freeman by conspiring with a Freeman who, for a consideration, would then vouch that the goods were his own property. Clearly it would have a detrimental effect on the revenue of the town and the King's customs or excise. How common such a practice may have been at different times it is impossible to say as in the great majority of cases the fraud would remain undiscovered, but it must be remembered that at various periods during the middle ages standards of honesty were very different from those now considered indispensable (even if not always observed). From the very fact that it is included in the Freemen's oath we may deduce that it must at some period have been both important and fairly widespread.

The requirement to observe all lawful ordinances made by common consent on High Court days means that the Freeman is to conduct himself in accordance with the bye-laws of the City but the wording of the phrase is interesting. The oath has already required obedience to the Mayor, Aldermen, Sheriff and all other civic officers (i.e. the Common Council) and the Court of Guild. This clause seems to refer to the Ordinances made by the Mayor and Burgesses in Guild assembled as authorised by the Town's Charters. The reference to High Court Days means the same, as we find frequently referred to in the town's documents as Full Courts or Full Guilds, that is the three meetings in each year held at Michaelmas, Christmas and Easter at which it was the duty of all Burgesses to attend.

The final clause covers the general military and civil duties of a Freeman that is to bear his share of the town's burdens and to play his appropriate part as a freeman in its organisation.

Wallis in his History of Northumberland 1769[4] gives a somewhat different and more lengthy form of oath. His accounts of the Courts and practices in Newcastle were severely criticised by Nathaniel Punshon, an Attorney at Law and Under-Sheriff and it must be admitted that Wallis's information concerning the Courts at least seems to have been very inaccurate.[5] Punshon, who was in a position to know the current practice at the time Brand's History was published, must be regarded as more reliable. The form of Oath given by Wallis has the appearance of being authentic and it seems improbable that he would invent it. It is possible that he has preserved an older form of oath (his form contains matter that looks archaic), or alternatively that he has used the form of oath applicable to some other town. Wallis's form reads as follows:

> "Ye shall swear that ye shall be good and true to our Sovereign Lord King George III and to the heirs of our Sovereign Lord the King obeisant and obedient ye shall be to the Mayor and Ministers of the Corporation the Franchises and customs thereof ye shall maintain and this town keep harmless in that you is. You shall be contributory to all manner of charges within this town as summons watches contributions taxes tallages lot scot and to all other charges bearing your part as a freeman ought to do Ye shall colour no foreign goods under or in your name whereby the King or this town might or may lose their customs or advantages Ye shall know no foreigner to buy or sell any merchandise with any foreigner within this corporation or franchise thereof but ye shall warn the Mayor thereof or some ministering under him Ye shall implead or sue no freeman out of this town whilst you may have right and law within the same town Ye shall take no apprentice but if he be free born that is to say no

---

[4] Vol II p200.

[5] Brand II p190 n.

bondmans son nor the child of an alien and for no less term than for seven years without fraud or deceit and within the first year ye shall cause him to be enrolled or else pay such fine as shall reasonably be imposed upon you for omitting the same and after his term's end within convenient time being required ye shall make him free of the Corporation if he have well and truly served you Ye shall also keep the King's peace in your own person Ye shall know no gatherings conventicles nor conspiracies against the King's peace but ye shall warn the Mayor thereof or let it to your power All these points and articles ye shall well and truly keep according to the laws and customs of this corporation to your power So God You Help".

The Great Charter of Queen Elizabeth decreed that the admission of Burgesses should be carried out either by the Mayor and Burgesses (i.e. the Court of Guild) or the Mayor and Common Council. In the seventeenth and eightenth centuries the function seems to have been shared between the two bodies in so far as the applicants for the freelage had to be approved by the Court of Guild but their admissions were regulated by order of the Common Council and the actual ceremony of admission was carried out either by the Mayor or one of the Aldermen or the Sheriff. The Common Council ceased to exist on the passing of the Municipal Corporations Act 1835 but that Act did not affect the Court of Guild except in so far as its functions were inconsistent with the Act. There seems to be nothing in the Act which is in any way inconsistent with the Court of Guild dealing with the whole process of admission, and perhaps therefore some legal power of continuing, amending or dispensing with the Freeman's Oath still continued in the Court of Guild.

The Local Government Act 1972 (effective as at 1st April, 1974) made the Lord Mayor responsible for examining the claim of any person to be admitted but did not specify any admission ceremony. The Act does however continue the rights of Freemen as they were on 31st March 1974, from which it would seem that a new Freeman whose claim has been established is entitled to be admitted by the traditional ceremony, including the Declaration in the same terms as the former oath. The Town Moor Act 1988 confirmed the powers of the Court of Guild to regulate all matters affecting the Freemen, with some exceptions but including admission, from which it seems that the former power of the Mayor and Burgesses and old Common Council to remove a "stop" continues in the Court of Guild.

CHAPTER 7

The Duties and Privileges of Freemen

This survey of the duties and privileges of Freemen is divided into two periods - before and after 1836. In that year the duties of Freemen as such came to an end together with most of the surviving privileges. The political agitation which led up to the Municipal reforms of 1835 concentrated perhaps too much on what were thought to be the privileges and advantages of being a Freeman while the duties and liabilities were overlooked. It is, however, true that the duties and liabilities which in earlier ages had been burdensome had been considerably alleviated whilst the rights and privileges were or could be valuable.

Before 1836

The earliest duties of which we know relating to Freemen or Burgesses of Boroughs were comprised in Anglo Saxon days under the heading of the Trinoda Necessitas. The three duties of the Saxon Burgess were to contribute to the building and maintenance of bridges, the building and maintenance of defences and service in the militia when called upon. We can trace these duties down through the centuries though naturally their form varied over the years. They reflect the civil and military duties of the Freemen and they also reflect the fact that these duties were those imposed on all free land holders so they may be found in manors as well as in boroughs. Throughout the mediaeval period it was common for fines for misdemeanours (or part of them) to be applied to the maintenance of the Tyne Bridges. The Norman bridge was destroyed by fire in 1248, and its replacement, by the great flood of 1771. The obligation of contributing to the local defences was reflected in the tax named murage (a toll levied to meet the cost of building the town walls), which was a source of complaint to the Burgesses of Newcastle for a very long period from the thirteenth to the sixteenth centuries. Service in the militia in defence of the country or of the King's peace was not merged in the military system of feudalism, but as a national system of defence it was so clumsy as to be almost useless. The feudal levies and the mercenaries employed by the Normans were intensely unpopular and provoked great resistance from the English in the time of Stephen and it should not be forgotten that it was the English militia who defeated the Scots in the Battle of the Standard 1138 and successfully resisted the Scottish invasion. We do not know precisely who the soldiers were who rode from Newcastle to capture William the Lion in 1174 but it is not unreasonable to suppose that some at least of them were Burgesses of Newcastle. Henry II's Assize of Arms 1181 prescribed that "all Burgesses and the whole community of Freemen must have a tunic and iron sword and lance". This Royal Decree also laid down that those who had not these weapons must provide them whilst those who had more should sell them to someone who would use them in the King's service. The travelling Justices were to oversee by means of sworn juries of Freemen of the boroughs the carrying out of this Decree, which was to be read to the Burgesses at their common audience. Also all the bearers of arms were to swear to use them in the King's service and none but a Freeman was to be admitted to this oath, i.e. the bearing of arms was limited to Freemen. The Assize of Arms was repeated by Henry III in an extended form and in conjunction with the system of watch and ward was carried down by subsequent legislation of Edward I, Henry IV, Philip and Mary and James I in principle up to modern times. In Newcastle particularly, which was always in the forefront of the Scottish Wars, military service in defence of the town was one of the primary obligations of the Freemen. It was also normal practice for successive sovereigns to call upon Newcastle to provide ships and men for naval service and on occasions Newcastle provided a not inconsiderable fleet. The Shipwrights of Newcastle built one of Edward I's galleys. We do not know by whom it was manned but it seems highly probable that the first crew would be drawn from the Port of Tyne.

The civil duties of a burgess was first of all to be responsible for payment of his share of the town's taxes (see appendix 3) and secondly to undertake the burden of holding office when elected by his fellow Burgesses. In modern days we regard the holding of civic office as a privilege to be sought but in mediaeval times the expense of holding office could be ruinous to the holder, so much so that some would elect to pay the heavy fines incurred by refusal rather than accept the office. These fines were expressly provided in the Charters of Elizabeth and James I but the Charters were probably only setting out what was accepted local custom. Presumably in Newcastle there were sufficient Burgesses of substance and standing who were prepared to accept the various offices.

Apart from the advantages of their exclusive rights to carry on trades and crafts, which died out in the eighteenth century, the great privilege of the Burgesses was freedom from toll of various kinds. This was first granted by Charter of Henry II in 1175 and continued until the death of the last surviving Freeman admitted by service as an apprentice who had been in such service in or before 1836. Probably, therefore, it continued in existence up to about a century ago. Clearly in times when Newcastle was a staple town for various commodities, in particular wool, this privilege would be extremely valuable to the local merchants who were Freemen. Certainly it became very valuable to the Hostmen who carried on the coal trade. Before the age of statistics it is difficult to assess just how valuable such a privilege could be but the figures produced to the Parliamentary Commissioners at their enquiry in 1833 reveal something of how it could place the Freeman merchant at an advantage over his non-freeman competitor.

The Freemen also had rights of pasturage not only on Newcastle Town Moor but also in the adjoining manors of Byker, Jesmond and Elswick. The rights over adjoining manors seem quietly to have disappeared even before the end of the Scottish Wars but those on the Town Moor still remain. These grazing rights came to be regarded in the eighteenth and nineteenth centuries as a form of provision for the poorer Freemen and their widows and although the richer Freemen may have been entitled to grazing, they did not in fact make use of such rights. Similarly, there were almshouses and charities for the relief of poverty provided for Freemen and their dependants. These will be dealt with in the chapter relating to charities.

Another important privilege of the Freemen prior to 1832 was that of selecting and electing the members of Parliament for the town. Edward I was the first King to call Parliaments with any degree of regularity and he required the Burgesses of each borough to send two representatives to his Parliaments which met at different towns and cities such as Westminster, Winchester and York. In 1283 Edward I sent a letter to, amongst others, the Mayor and Bailiffs of Newcastle upon Tyne, requiring them to cause two of the wiser and more suitable citizens to attend a national council at Shrewsbury. Representatives of towns were not called to the Councils or Parliaments held in 1290 and 1294 but they were summoned from the boroughs for the Parliament held in 1295 at Westminster. The King's writ to the Sheriff specifies two Burgesses from each borough within his jurisdiction and Newcastle was duly represented by Hugh of Carliol and Peter Graper. From this time forward it was customary, whenever the Parliament was summoned, that two Burgesses should be elected by the Burgesses of Newcastle to represent them. Those who elected the members of Parliament were the Burgesses who were entitled to attend the meetings of the full Guild and thus a right of voting for MP's came to be vested in the Freemen at large. Non-Freemen, of course, had no vote. This continued to be the voting position until the Reform Act of 1832 when although the Freemen continued to be entitled to vote as Freemen the electorate was enlarged by the addition of the forty shilling freeholders so the Freemen's exclusive rights had gone.

Another privilege prior to 1836 was that Freemen alone were eligible for all the offices of the town corporation except the Recorder and were alone entitled to elect these officials.

After the Municipal Corporations Act 1835

This Act (effective 1836), the wording and effect of which is far from clear, repealed all statutes, charters, usages and customs which were inconsistent with its terms and set up a new system of local government in the principal boroughs of England and Wales as scheduled in the Act. It did not apply to London, Alnwick and some other boroughs which therefore retained their then existing systems. The Act threw open to all the right of trading thus bringing to an end the Freemen's trading monopoly. It also abolished their exclusive rights of holding office in the town and of electing the civic office holders and officials. The right to freedom from tolls was preserved to existing Freemen and their apprentices then bound. It did not take away Freemen's individual rights or their eligibility to participate in charities restricted to themselves but property belonging to the Freemen as part of the corporate body was transferred to the ownership of the new Town Council set up under the Act. Similarly, the Act did not affect the rights of Freemen's Companies or the organisation of Freemen amongst themselves nor the property held by Freemen's Companies irrespective of whether they were formally incorporated or not. The promoters of the Act had originally intended to abolish the Freemen altogether but this was or would have been an immensely complicated operation which would have interfered very seriously with the rights of individuals. After much heated debate the Act ultimately preserved the Freemen though prohibiting admission by purchase or gift.

The 1835 Act was followed by further Municipal Corporations Acts in 1882 and 1883. These did not affect the principle adopted by the earlier Act, which, although repealed, was in effect re-enacted so far as the Freemen were concerned. These Acts were followed by the Local Government Act 1933, which again maintained the same principle, re-enacting it in different words: this was again repealed by the Local Government Act 1972 but re-enacted in a different form which preserves the status and rights of the Freemen and their successors. Like the 1835 Act the 1972 Act had started out to abolish Freemen altogether, but the forceful representations of Freemen themselves from various towns and cities, amongst which Newcastle was prominent, were effective in securing the insertion of appropriate clauses to achieve the result.

At the present time the prime duty of a Freeman is to make sure that the Town Moor is properly managed and maintained as an open space, free of encroachment and unlawful enclosure in accordance with the Town Moor Act 1988. If necessary he can attend the Court of Guild and address the Lord Mayor drawing attention to his complaint. (This may of course be regarded as a privilege as well as a duty!) The remaining privileges are (a) for resident Freemen and widows of Freemen the right to graze two cows on the Town Moor or to participate in the stint money (see chapter 9 on Town Moor) and (b) for Freemen and their dependants the eligibility to receive assistance from the various Freemen's charities (see chapters 10 and 11 on Charities). The remaining duties, rights and privileges are therefore of little material value but the Freemen and their families and apprentices still place a great, though non-material, value on their right to be Freemen and the guardianship of the Town Moor.

CHAPTER 8

The Guildhall, Thornton's Hospital and The Blackfriars

The Guildhall and Thornton's Hospital

Some authorities have ascribed the foundation of the Guildhall to Roger Thornton, one of Newcastle's most distinguished Burgesses, but it would seem that he cannot have been the founder. He did, in fact, found an Almshouse, known as Thornton's Hospital (otherwise the Maison Dieu), the site, or part of it, adjoining the east end of the Guildhall. This foundation may have caused confusion.

The first reference at present known to a Guildhall in Newcastle occurs in a document[1] witnessed by "John of the Gildehalle". This document is undated but is estimated to be between 1240-1250. Towards the end of the thirteenth century the will of one Milisand Godfrey[2] refers to a street or lane towards "Aulam Ghylde" and there are a number of references in the first quarter of the fourteenth century. The Royal Charters of 1345 and 1400 mention the Guildhall.

These references show clearly that there must have been a Guildhall in existence long before Roger Thornton's period. None of them, however, throws any light on the geographical position of the Guildhall but this can be established from Thornton's foundation charter of the Almshouse which is stated to be bounded on the west by the Guildhall.

In 1402 Thornton obtained a royal licence to convey to the Mayor and Commonalty a site for his proposed almshouse, which was also a religious establishment, later known as Thornton's Hospital or St Katherine's Hospital or the Maison Dieu. In 1412 another royal licence was obtained to incorporate the newly built hospital and on St Katherine's day 1425 Thornton executed a foundation and endowment charter.[3] The hospital survived until 1656 or shortly after but

---

[1] END No 15, p 19.

[2] Brand I p 210.

[3] AA3 vol XIV p191.

the east part of its building lasted until 1823, when it was pulled down and a new building erected on its site.

The old Guildhall, having survived some four centuries, had been pulled down by the corporation in 1655 and a new Guildhall built on the site by the architect Robert Trollop, of York, and this has survived, with various alterations (including some by John Dobson) over the years, until the present time.

The upper floor of the Maison Dieu, which had been the meeting place of the Merchant Companies from the late fifteenth century (or perhaps earlier), was pulled down in 1823 but the Merchant Adventurers Court on its upper floor was reinstated in exactly the same position, including its magnificent oak panelling and the fireplace with its overmantel and the elaborate plaster ceiling which bears the date 1636 in the corners of its central panel. The principal entrance to the Merchant Adventurers Court is a fine doorway leading directly from the upper floor of the Guildhall.

Edward III's Charter of 1345 directed that an amended form of electing the Mayor should be carried out in the Guildhall.[4] Henry IV's Charter of 1400 directed that the new courts set up when Newcastle was made a county of itself were to be held in the Guildhall. In fact the Mayor's Court and the Sheriff's Court were held in the Guildhall from this time until they were abandoned in the nineteenth century when the County Court was established.

The Guildhall contains the large seventeenth century court. From it, entrance is obtained to a smaller room, known as the Towns Chamber, but better known now as The Lord Mayor's Parlour. In this room for some two centuries the Lord Mayor, Sheriff, Aldermen and Common Council met and transacted the business of the government of the town. It is also the meeting place of the Hostmen's Company, who were directed by Queen Elizabeth's Great Charter to hold their meetings in the Guildhall on the 4th January every year.

The Blackfriars

The Priory of the Dominican or Black Friars was established

---

[4] Brand II p161.

in Newcastle about 1238-39 and was occupied by them until the dissolution. The Priory Church was retained by the Crown and the remaining buildings were sold to the Mayor and Burgesses of Newcastle in 1544.[5] In 1552 the buildings, with the surrounding orchards and gardens, were granted to the nine Companies of Freemen in whom, with the three Merchant Companies, the right to elect the Mayor, Sheriff, Aldermen, Common Council and civic officials was vested (the Merchant Companies met in the Merchant Adventurers Court adjoining the Guildhall). The nine companies who were granted the Blackfriars buildings were the Bakers and Brewers, the Fullers and Dyers, the Smiths, the Tanners, the Butchers, the Cordwainers, the Saddlers, the Taylors and the Skinners and Glovers. The buildings were divided up into nine meeting halls for the companies but were purchased by the Corporation of Newcastle from the companies in the second half of the twentieth century so that the whole could be restored. Some of the halls have been adapted to other purposes but the Smiths Hall has been retained as a meeting place for the Freemen's Companies and as an example of their medieval past. This hall is still used by the Freemen.

It is worth noticing that the Friars occupied the buildings from about 1240 until 1544, roughly three centuries, but the Freemen's Companies were in occupation from 1555 up to 1955 or later and were, therefore, in occupation for a century longer than the Friars.

[5] Brand I pp132, 133.

CHAPTER 9

The Town Moor

Bourne in his History of Newcastle recorded a tradition that the Town Moor had in ancient times been an oak forest and the trees had been used to build ships and houses in ancient Newcastle. There is no known evidence to support this alleged tradition, which upon consideration appears somewhat improbable. Much more probable is the explanation given by Dr Dendy in a lecture[1] to the Literary and Philosphical Society of Newcastle upon Tyne in which he said that the town or village would in Anglo-Saxon times have been organised on the well-known three-field system, consisting of arable fields adjacent to the village, beyond them some hay meadows called leazes (grazed after the hay crop had been taken at Lammas), and beyond these the common pastures. This explanation although based purely on analogy, for there is no direct evidence, appears somewhat more probable than the tradition reported by Bourne.

The expression "Town Moor" strictly speaking refers to the part formerly known as the Castle Moor but has, since the middle of the seventeenth century, been used as a term comprising the entire area, consisting of the fields and moors known in medieval times as the Castle Field, Castle Leazes, Castle Moor and Nuns Moor. As the boundaries of these areas are in some cases unknown and have been altered at various times, it is impossible to define them with accuracy. The total area at the end of the seventeenth century would seem to have been about 1229 acres. No change seems to have taken place from that time up to 1870, when the area was stated in the Newcastle Improvement Act to be 1226 acres or thereabouts. Since 1870 there have been some substantial changes in the course of which the Freemen have given up some areas of Town Moor land and in many cases received other land in exchange. These will be referred to later.

---

[1] 11th October 1909. Printed in Lit & Phil Lectures 1921.

Despite its considerable commercial and trading interests the town of Newcastle remained, until at least the middle of the eighteenth century, a largely rural community accommodated within its town walls. In 1653 the Common Council of the Burgesses employed a neatherd and his staff to collect the Burgesses' cows every morning, drive them out to the Town Moor, supervise them and return them to the town each evening.[2] At that time about half the area within the town walls was still open ground, gardens, orchards and the like, and there was evidently pressure upon the land available for pasture for the cows which induced the Common Council to buy back considerable areas which had fallen into private ownership, namely the Nuns Moor and parts of Castle Leazes, thus restoring (though perhaps not in full) the area of the original town pastures. The Nuns Moor belonged to the nunnery of St Bartholomew in Newcastle from the time of Henry I until after the Dissolution.

Some of the boundaries being uncertain, and areas estimated rather than measured, it is impossible to give accurate figures for the extent of the Town Moor lands as a whole.

The following is an approximation:

Town Moor	848 acres
Nuns Moor	240 acres
Castle Leazes, including Castle Field	141 acres
	1229 acres[3]

This corresponds, within a reasonable margin of error, with the figure of 1226 acres mentioned in the Newcastle Improvement Act 1870.

In 1771 and indeed earlier, the Freemen were becoming concerned about encroachments on the Moor particularly the grant of wayleaves and the construction of roads. Following the

---

[2] Common Council Minute Book 1st April 1653. For later rules see Freemans Pocket Companion p78 Also the Stewards Rules and Orders 1888/9.

[3] Figures given by Brand, Bourne, & R Nichol's plan 1809.

Easter Guild in 1771, the Stewards of the Companies appointed a committee to examine the rights by which any roads over the Town Moor were enjoyed, and the Town Clerk's records. It was further agreed that the land lying west of the road to Cowgate ought to be improved, and that the Common Council should be petitioned to deal with these matters. The investigation revealed some agreements with owners of the Kenton and Coxlodge Grounds whereby they accepted responsibility for maintaining the boundary hedge between the Nuns Moor and Town Moor and their respective lands, and had wayleave over the Town Moor from Fenham to a gate situated approximately where the south end of the present Kenton Road crosses the Town Moor boundary. Also revealed was an ancient dispute about a gate, called the Slaty Gate,[4] situated on what is now Fenham Hall Drive some two hundred and twenty yards from its junction with Ponteland Road. The Stewards were ultimately informed that the roadway leading over the Moor between Coxlodge, Kenton and Fenham had been granted by Acts of Common Council and that a Committee of the Common Council had been appointed to view the unimproved parts of the Town Moor and consider the best means to cultivate and improve these.[5]

This proposal gave rise to a chain of events of very far reaching importance. The Stewards heard no more of their suggestion, but on the 31st December 1771 the part of the Town Moor lying on the West side of the Western Turnpike Road from Gallowgate Quarry to the West Cowgate, containing about eighty-nine acres, was advertised by order of the Common Council to be let for the purpose of being cultivated and improved. The Stewards and the Freemen generally had for somewhile been very suspicious of the Common Council. They thought, perhaps quite rightly, that the Common Council was claiming power to deal with the surface of the Town Moor without regard to the Freemen's rights, and that the proposal which the Stewards had put forward was not being taken up in the manner they had intended. The Freemen, therefore,

---

[4] "Gate" in this context probably has its Ancient meaning, i.e. a roadway.

[5] Stewards Report etc printed by I Thompson 1771.

openly opposed the proceedings of the Common Council, which treated their opposition with contempt. The Council enclosed and let the land and the lessee fenced and built some kind of house on the land. The Freemen summoned meetings of the Companies, subscribed money and agreed to take the matter to Court. They chose a committee for this purpose, and sent formal notice to the Common Council and lessee that they intended to commit sufficient damage for them to ground an action of trespass, if it could be proved. They pulled down part of the fence and broke a gate (and according to one account pulled down the house) whereupon the lessee, supported by the Common Council, took legal proceedings. Attempts were made to compromise the dispute, but these proved ineffective and the matter came to trial at the Assizes on 10th August 1773. The Freemen persuaded Sergeant Glynn (the Recorder of London, a very distinguished barrister) to appear for them. He put forward a thorough and excellent defence to which the plaintiffs' counsel was unable to reply. It had become clear that the Council could not support their claim, so the matter was then disposed of by the judge's agreement to the withdrawal of a juror and an agreed rule of court by which the Council gave up their claims and submitted to pay £300 costs, and further that an Act of Parliament should be jointly solicited at the Corporation's expense to enable the burgesses to let the land for improvement, the rent to be divided by the Stewards of the respective companies amongst their poor brethren and widows. There was considerable difficulty in agreeing the precise terms of the proposed Act, but this was ultimately achieved and the result was the Town Moor Act 1774.[6]

This Act confirmed and established to the resident Freemen or Burgesses of Newcastle upon Tyne and the resident widows of deceased Freemen for ever the full right and benefit of the herbage of the Town Moor, Castle Leazes and Nuns Moor for two milk cows respectively in the accustomed manner. Subject to various restrictions, it was further enacted that for the purpose of improving the Town

[6] Freemans Pocket Companion p53.

Moor, leases could from time to time be made, not to exceed a hundred acres at any one time. The rents of such leases were to be paid to the Chamber Clerk of the Town and when they amounted to £100 or more he should pay them to a person appointed by the Stewards who were to distribute the money amongst the poor resident Freemen and widows as they should think fit.

This system for the collection and distribution of the rents continued in operation until 1970, when the system, although substantially remaining the same, was reorganised by a scheme of the Charity Commissioners under which the money is distributed by a body of Trustees appointed by the Stewards of the Companies. The leased areas (mostly playing fields or allotments) are known as Intakes and the distribution is officially styled the Town Moor Money Charity.

One of the results of the Town Moor Act 1774 was that the Stewards of the different Companies formed themselves into an association to watch over the Town Moor and the other rights and privileges of the Burgesses at large. In the years following the Act, it was found to have various disadvantages and in the early years of the nineteenth century suggestions were made, from time to time, that a new Act should be obtained to overcome the difficulties. A Select committee was unofficially appointed to go into the question. This committee negotiated with the Town Clerk and a draft bill was prepared, but before it could be launched in Parliament it was strongly opposed by some Freemen, who considered that the activities of the committee had not been properly made known to them. This gave rise to some undignified wrangling between the parties (the politics of the day being involved) when ultimately the authority, if any, of the Select committee was withdrawn, and the proposed bill discontinued.[7] The report of the committee was full of self justification but an account of the proceedings in Guild reveal the objections of the Freemen to the proposals. In particular, they objected to giving the Common Council power to mortgage parts of the Town Moor

---

[7] Freemens Pocket Companion pp 63 et seq. Select Commitee Report in Northumberland. & Newcastle Monthly Magazine 1818 at Lit. & Phil. Library.

which they considered would ultimately result in loss of their rights, and a proposal to reduce the amount of money payable out of the rents to the poor resident Freemen and widows which also would in the course of time destroy the Charity. One interesting aspect of the matter is that it was an instance of the Court of Guild (the Mayor and Burgesses assembled) exercising its powers under the charters of Elizabeth I and James I, which powers the Commmon Council was wont to allege no longer existed. It is also interesting as an early example of the system of dual control which has done so much to preserve the Town Moor as open spacc.

At the Christmas Guild 1808, a resolution had been proposed and carried to appoint a committee for the purpose of looking after the Freemen's interests in the Town Moor, but the Mayor had ruled (incorrectly) that the Court of Guild had no power to do this and the matter did not proceed, though shortly afterwards the unofficial Select committee engaged itself in the preparation of the proposed new Town Moor Act mentioned above which it considered was essential in order to improve the Moor. This proposal having been soundly defeated and the Committee having been dismissed at the Michaelmas Guild 1811, another committee was appointed by the Stewards of the Companies at the Easter Guild 1812 "solely for the better improvement of the Town Moor lands" - evidently as a result of the discontinuance of the Select committee. It was named the Herbage Committee and was re-elected by the Stewards at each succesive Guild. Its first report was rendered at the Michaelmas Guild 1812, detailing considerable work done during the summer, in clearing, draining, levelling, manuring and erecting cottages for the men employed on the Moor. The Herbage Committee continued to exercise its function until the Newcastle Improvement Act of 1870 changed its name to the Stewards Committee and enlarged its powers and responsibilities. The Town Moor Act 1988 further enlarged its duties and responsibilities and it continues to operate effectively in the management of the Moor.

Political reform was very active in the years after Waterloo. After the great Reform Act 1832 the Government set up a Commission to enquire into the existing state of the Municipal Corporations in England and Wales. The Commissioners came to Newcastle on 29th October 1833 and spent the ensuing ten days investigating the affairs of the Newcastle Corporation in considerable depth. The Town Clerk, Mr John Clayton, stated that the soil and mines of the Town Moor and Leazes belonged to the Corporation at large but the right to the herbage was given by Act of Parliament to the resident Burgesses and widows. He also reported that there was coal under the Town Moor which was then unwrought.[8] The subsequent Municipal Corporations Act 1835 abolished the old Common Council and set up a new Town Council. This Act gave rise to some difficulty of interpretation and the question arose between the Town Council and the Freemen as to who should pay for the upkeep of the Town Moor, payment having previously been made by the old Corporation out of Corporate revenue. It was ultimately agreed that the Corporation should pay to the Stewards an annual sum of £400 for this purpose. This sum was paid from about 1836 up to 1988 when the finances were reorganised.

For a very long period in the eighteenth and ninetenth centuries, there had been tension between the Freemen in general and the Common Council of the town, the members of which were Freemen themselves, but who tended to regard the Town Moor from a different angle. The reformed Town Council, consisting of ratepayers many of whom were Freemen, continued to have thoughts and make suggestions that the Town Moor should be developed in various ways so as to produce revenue for the town which was rapidly increasing in size. There was also much pressure and a long campaign to convert the Town Moor into a public park. Ultimately, the Newcastle Improvement Act of 1870 authorised the Corporation to take two areas, each not exceeding thirty-five acres in the Castle Leazes and Town Moor. These two areas

---

[8] Proceedings of the Court of Enquiry, published by Newcastle Journal 15th January 1834, p115.

were duly set apart and are still maintained as public parks known as Leazes Park and Exhibition Park respectively. Later Acts authorised the construction of the Nuns Moor Park and Brandling Park. A number of main roads have also been constructed, notably Claremont Road, Grandstand Road, Nuns Moor Road and the North West radial road. A considerable area was also taken for the site of the Royal Victoria Infirmary (1898) and its adjoining orthopaedic hospital (1917) and in the 1970's developments first of the Dental Hospital and School and then the University Medical School. Further land has been taken for the construction of the University Halls of Residence.

No land was substituted for the areas taken for public parks and roads but in nearly all other cases substituted land has been obtained. There are thus outlying parts of Town Moor land situated at Coxlodge, Fawdon and Little Benton Farm which is situated in the east side of Newcastle. The Freemen have sometimes been criticised on the grounds that they have failed adequately to defend the Town Moor land against encroachment. This criticism however seems to have little justification for the total areas taken out of Town Moor lands since 1770 (apart from minor boundary adjustments) is about two hundred and ten acres against which some sixty acres have been added as exchange land. The net decrease in area is therefore about a hundred and fifty acres (roughly 12% of the original total). All this, however, is still public land and open space, being about a hundred acres of parks and fifty acres of main roads. Set against a background of the enormous increase in the size of the town of Newcastle in the last two hundred years, the decrease in the total area seems relatively modest. There can be little doubt that had it not been for the insistence by the Freemen on maintaining their rights over this open space it, or at least a very large part, would have succumbed to development and been utilised for factories and residential estates.

The expression "dual control" has been used to describe the somewhat unusual combination of ownership of the soil and minerals by one party and the surface by another, having the effect that neither can do anything very much without the consent of the other.

No mention has been made of other matters relating to the Town Moor which may be of interest. The first of these is the history of the Barracks. In 1794 the Army obtained permission from the Freemen to erect a military depot and barracks on the Castle Leazes, adjoining the Turnpike Road to Cowgate. These barracks were subsequently extended in the 1914-18 War to include infantry and artillery barracks. Most of the site of these barracks has been given up by the Ministry of Defence at intervals after 1960 but part is still retained for use of the territorial army, although the rest of the site, which was quite unsuitable for restoration as grass land, has been redeveloped chiefly for use by public corporations. The whole site however remains part of the Town Moor.

A large section of the central area of the Town Moor was used from the middle of the eighteenth century up to 1883 as a racecourse. The mid-summer race meeting held in the last full week in June every year was immensely popular and was accompanied, as such races usually are, by travelling shows and booths who paid small rents to the Freemen. When the race meeting was transferred to Gosforth Park it was decided to hold a Temperance Festival every year at the same time in order to provide entertainment (other than alcoholic) to the large numbers who used race week as an annual holiday. Thus was instituted the Temperance Festival which has continued since its inception. It has grown out of all recognition and is now said to be the largest travelling fairground in the British Isles and possibly in the whole of Europe, though the name Temperance has now been omitted from its title. It is known as the 'Hoppings' and the site covers some 40 acres.

In the early years of the twentieth century, it had become a practice to bring large roundabouts and other travelling shows on to the Moor, being towed behind heavy traction engines which caused damage to the herbage. In 1912 the damage caused by these vehicles was very substantial indeed. The Stewards Committee therefore objected to any repetition of this in 1913 although they did not object to the customary military and civilian sports. The City Council took it upon themselves to authorise the showmen's vehicles to enter on the Town Moor, as a result of which further very substantial damage was done. This was in effect a re-assertion by the Corporation of the City of rights which their predecessors had asserted in 1771. The Stewards Committee took action against the showmen who were supported by the Corporation. The case came on for trial in May 1914, when the Freemen's rights were again upheld in full. The Corporation then appealed but were again defeated.[9] Since this decision the Freemen's rights have not been challenged though in 1948 there was a proposal by one party of the City Council to buy them out. This was really a party political move which was dropped when the political control of the Council changed. The proposal had however served a useful purpose in so far as it demonstrated that there was much misunderstanding between the Council and the Freemen. The Chairman of the Freemen, Mr Lorne Robson, determined to improve this situation and arranged to meet the Chairman of the Council's Town Moor and Parks Committee monthly on an informal basis in order to avoid disputes. This developed after a few years into the setting up of a joint committee of representatives of the Stewards' Committee and the Town Moor and Parks Committee to discuss matters affecting both parties.

This joint committee, now known as the Town Moor Joint Management Sub-Committee, meets regularly and has achieved great success in avoiding or settling any differences.

As mentioned earlier, a number of gypsies and miscellaneous booths and sideshows used to come onto the Town Moor during the race meeting, and were charged small fees. The number of these was very modest and little objection, if any, was raised. When the races were moved to Gosforth Park in 1882 itinerants continued as before but were not part of the Temperance Festival. The number of these itinerants increased over the years and they became a real nuisance causing much environmental damage. An important milestone in the history of the Freemen was set when action was taken to deal with what

---

[9] Walker v. Murphy L.J. (1914) Ch.917

was an act of trespass by these itinerants. This built up to a very substantial problem and indeed a public nuisance amounting in 1986 to some 600 vehicles trespassing on the Moor. The very future of the traditional 'Hoppings' was threatened. The City Council were unco-operative over measures to exclude the itinerants and the Showmen's Guild of Great Britain sought assistance from the Freemen to resolve the matter. In 1987 the Stewards' Committee engaged the services of a Security firm (at considerable expense) and no itinerant traveller gained acces onto a Moor under the control of the Freemen. At the insistence of the the City Council they were allowed onto the Little Moor for which the City had an Agreement in lieu of Stints. As the City had not adhered to the Agreement, the Stewards' Committee consequently decided not to renew, thus retaining possession of the grazing. Despite a security pass operation in 1990 six itinerant families gained access to the Town Moor.

The Town Moor Act 1988 enabled the Freemen to take court action. The matter was heard at the Moot Hall before His Honour Judge George Hall. In his summary Judge Hall condemned the City Council for their lack of action against the itinerants who were not welcome and had caused local residents much grief. He congratulated the Freemen on their action and found in their favour with immediate eviction and costs. Following court action there has been no trespass by unauthorised persons onto the Town Moor. In 1991 and 1992 the Freemen made a concession to the City and allowed twenty families to use an area of Hunters Moor. In 1993 the City did not request the use of Town Moor land and provided an extra itinerant site on the outskirts of the City. Itinerants, rather than the genuine gypsies associated with the fairground, are no longer able to gain access to any of the moors. In 1994 and 1995 no itinerant arrived in Newcastle with the intention of trespassing on any of the moors, however the security measures will continue for some years to come.

The Local Government Act 1972 included two clauses which affected the Freemen. One was to preserve the Freemen's status and property rights generally and the other was to repeal all local legislation. This expression was so defined that it would include not only the Town Moor Act of 1774 but also very numerous clauses in other Newcastle upon Tyne Acts. Shortly after the Local Government Act came into force on 1st April 1974, the Stewards' Committee agreed with the City Council that the appropriate way to deal with the situation was to promote a new Town Moor Act to re-establish beyond doubt the Freemen's role and rights to ensure that the Town Moor remained free of encroachments, to establish proper financial arrangements between parties and to regulate and modernise the good management of the Town Moor as an asset, i.e. the 'city lung'.

The basic principles of the new Act were agreed very early in the discussions but the details were found to be much more complicated than expected. It took several years of work to draft and obtain the approval of the Charity Commissioners and a range of Government Departments. When laid before Parliament it was delayed by the vagaries of Parliamentary procedure and particularly by certain politicians who, having no interest whatever the matter, wished to use it to further projects of their own.

The Stewards' Committee had been careful to keep the Stewards of the Incorporated Companies fully informed of the various measures proposed and the reasons for them, thus avoiding the fate of the Select Committee of 1809. The Bill was finally approved by Parliament and received Royal assent on 20th December 1988. It is officially named the Newcastle upon Tyne Town Moor Act 1988 Cap XXXI. The enactments repealed are shown in Appendix VII.

The work done in securing this Act covering a period of some fifteen years was carried through primarily by Mrs Valerie A Dodds (City Council) and Messrs Robert K Dotchin, Robin F Walker, Alan T Alderson and Leonard R Fenwick (all Chairmen of the Feemen). In addition there can be no doubt that without the assistance of Mr. Nicholas H Brown, MP for Newcastle East, the Act may well have foundered and not reached the Statue Book. All these deserve appreciation not only from the Freemen but also from the citizens of Newcastle and indeed from the public at large for whose benefit the Town Moor continues in greater part to be maintained as open space.

CHAPTER 10

The St Mary Magdalene
and Holy Jesus Trust

The present St Mary Magdalene and Holy Jesus Trust
(formerly Hospital) was formed by amalgamating in 1970 two
previously separate charitable organisations having very
different histories up to that time. These will be set out
separately. One observation should however be made here,
namely that the name hospital is now used to describe
institutions all having the treatment of medical illness or
accident as their object. In medieval times however the word
meant primarily a building or organisation for the care of the
aged or impotent, perhaps more in the nature of what we
should call now an almshouse or hospice. This distinction gave
rise to some confusion when the National Health Service
started and it became necessary to convince the Ministry of
Health that neither the St Mary Magdalene Hospital nor the
Holy Jesus Hospital were medical hospitals in the modern
sense but were in fact almshouses for the aged and poor
Freemen. The Holy Jesus Hospital had been founded for this
particular purpose but the St Mary Magdalene Hospital
originally had some connection with the medieval world of
medicine, providing a place for the residence of lepers, and
later when leprosy had died out, for victims of the plagues, as
well as providing for the reception of pilgrims travelling to St
Mary's chapel in Jesmond.

The Hospital of St Mary Magdalene

This hospital is said by Bourne (1736) and Brand (1789) to
have been founded by Henry I but neither quotes any
authority or reference. Possibly they were preserving an oral
tradition. It was described by them as a Priory or Hospital for a
Master, Brethren and Sisters to receive persons suffering from
leprosy. The earliest document[1] mentioning the Hospital is a
lease about 1220 of some premises subject to an annual

---

[1] E.N.D. No 190 p119.

burgage rent of one half penny to the King and a fixed payment to the Hospital. The rent to the landlord was eighteen silver pence. The amount of the royal rent as a burgage and the unspecified amount to the Hospital suggest that the foundation must be considered to be much older than the period of the lease. Another document relating to the hospital was a Papal Bull dated 4th March 1260-61 which confirmed to the Master and Brethren their present and future possessions.[2] Neither of these documents refers to the foundation of the hospital. The premises and chapel were extended or improved about the middle of the fourteenth century. Some of the buildings were still remaining when Brand wrote his history and indeed in 1830 when the old hospital situated between the present St Mary's Place and Vine Lane was pulled down. A replacement for the hospital was then built in a position a short distance to the north-west of the Hancock Museum. This new hospital was itself pulled down on being replaced by the present almshouses adjoining Claremont Road and Hunters Road in Spital Tongues.

The original hospital as a religious institution was dissolved by King Henry VIII in 1539 but apparently never came in charge before the King's auditors and in 1542 the Master and Brethren and Sisters granted a lease of the hospital for eighty-five years to Robert Brandling. It seems that the hospital was granted away by Queen Elizabeth in 1582 but was re-established by charter of King James I.

By this charter dated 12th June 1611 the chapel of St Thomas on the Tyne Bridge was incorporated with the Hospital of St Mary Magdalene, having presumably been a separate establishment. The preamble to the charter states that because the ancient deeds of endowment of the two places had been lost or destroyed and some persons were attempting to appropriate their possessions to their own use, the King amalgamated them as a corporate body named the Hospital of St Mary Magdalene, consisting of a Master and three old poor and unmarried Burgesses as a body politic in law, with a common seal power to sue and be sued to grant leases and

---

[2] Brand I p425.

manage the properties. The Mayor and Burgesses, i.e. the corporate body of the town, were to be the patrons of the reorganised hospital with the presentation of the mastership and power to review and alter the statutes. To what extent the hospital as an incorporated body managed its own affairs is not clear. Legal opinions were taken in 1721 as to the extent of the powers of the Master and Brethren to grant leases for periods of ten years or three lives. During many years before 1800 the Corporation of Newcastle purported to exercise a right of granting leases of the property of the Hospital but in that year the Master considered it his duty to resist the Corporation's usurpation of the right. The matter was litigated from 1800 to 1816 when the right of the Master and Brethren of the Hospital to lease their own property was established and the Corporation was adjudged to pay £3,500 for rents. The Hospital owned lands of quite considerable extent between the eastern end of Pandon Dean and Spital Tongues. The value of these lands increased very considerably as the town expanded and the income became more than sufficient to maintain the Master and Brethren. The Corporation had been authorised by an Act in 1786 to acquire the Chapel on the Tyne Bridge and when the Chapel ceased to be used for Divine Service in 1827 it was demolished and the site was sold to the Corporation. By an Act passed in 1828 the Hospital was required to utilise the proceeds of sale to build and maintain another Chapel on its land. Thus was built in 1830 the still existing Chapel of St Thomas the Martyr (now known as St Thomas's Church) between St Mary's Place and the present Civic Centre. The Hospital also in 1848 established St Thomas's Schools for the education of "the poorer classes of inhabitants". In 1867 a further Act reorganised the Hospital and authorised the establishment of an almshouse for sixteen Brethren and their wives and a house for the Master. It also provided for the application of surplus revenue to the establishment of a medical hospital for the poor. This was carried into effect by the setting up of the St Mary Magdalene Home for Incurables off Hunters Road, Spital Tongues, now called the Hunters Moor Hospital, taken over by the National Health Service in 1948.

The Holy Jesus Hospital

The Holy Jesus Hospital was an almshouse erected in 1682 by the Mayor and Burgesses for the sustentation and relief of poor Freemen and their widows and daughters. The building still stands in the Manors (City Road) and is now in use as the John Joicey Museum. It was designed to provide for forty residents and is of architectural interest, having been described by some experts as unique in England. Its history as an almshouse is perhaps unexceptional but the circumstances of its endowment and subsequent maintenance as a charitable institution though now largely forgotten are of sufficient interest to be summarized here.

In 1597 an Act of Parliament was passed (39 Elizabeth cap 5) described as an Act for erecting of Hospitals for the Poor. This Act was made perpetual by another Act in 1623. These Acts authorised the construction and endowment of almshouses for the poor which were to be organized as legally incorporated bodies managing their own affairs. In pursuance of this statutory authority the Mayor and Burgesses acting by the Common Council in 1683 built the Hospital of the Holy Jesus and by an indenture dated 26th March formally appointed that Thomas Lewen and thirty-nine others already placed in the hospital should be incorporated by the name of the Master, Brethren and Sisters of the Hospital of the Holy Jesus, to have continuance for ever with power to purchase and hold lands, goods and chattels, to sue in the courts and have a common seal. It further provided that the Common Council should have power to remove the Master or any of the Brethren or Sisters and to fill up vacancies and to make rules and orders for the governance of the Hospital. At the same time property in The Close, Newcastle (the site of the Mansion House) was conveyed to the Hospital, having been purchased by the Mayor and Burgesses for £700. In November 1683 the Mayor and Burgesses also purchased the Manor of Etherley, County Durham from Timothy Davison and Matthew Jeffreyson for £1,610. This property also was conveyed to the Hospital on 6th November 1683 and in September 1685 they purchased a farm known as Whittle at Shilbottle,

Northumberland from the same Timothy Davison and Matthew Jeffreyson for £1,300 which was conveyed to the Hospital.

In 1714 the Mayor and Burgesses decided to purchase the Walker Estate (then in Northumberland, though now in Newcastle). Not having sufficient funds available, they decided to raise some of the money required by selling the estates at Etherley and Whittle and to settle part of the Walker Estate on the Hospital in exchange, thus increasing the revenues available to support the Hospital. The purchase of the Walker Estate was carried through and the estates at Whittle and Etherley were sold by the Common Council, but the Brethren and the Sisters of the Hospital took no part in the transactions and the proceeds of sale of the estates were paid into the Corporation's general fund and not to the Hospital. It was alleged many years later that the Hospital had been consulted and had agreed to the sales, but this still seems somewhat open to doubt. The Common Council petitioned the House of Lords on 16th December 1716 for leave to bring in a Bill to authorise the sale of the estates at Etherley and Whittle and to settle part of the Walker Estate on the Hospital instead. The Council also presented a similar petition on behalf of the Master, Brethren and Sisters. Again it seems doubtful whether the Hospital actually agreed to this. The House of Lords however did not grant the necessary leave to bring in a Bill, apparently because their Lordships doubted whether the Corporate Body of Newcastle was authorised to act in this way. Further petitions were presented in the following session, giving more information, when leave was given and the Bill was brought in and read three times in the House of Lords. On the final debate however the Bill was not passed because the House was not satisfied that the Corporation had the necessary power, although the Corporation did produce the Town's Great Charter from Queen Elizabeth, one clause of which authorised the Corporation to purchase and hold lands notwithstanding the statutes of Mortmain. In spite of this the Corporation persuaded the purchasers of the estates at Etherley and Whittle to proceed, taking their conveyances from the Corporation and not from the Hospital. The Master, Brethren and Sisters took no part in these proceedings.

The Corporation completed its purchase of the Estate at Walker, but a claim was then made that the Estate was liable to be forfeited to the Crown because the Corporation had purchased it without obtaining the necessary licence and in defiance of the statutes of Mortmain. After much hard work by the members of Parliament, the Corporation was ultimately able to obtain the necessary licence in 1723 but although they had taken possession of the Walker Estate, they did not proceed with the proposed Act of Parliament to settle any part of it on the Hospital, nor did they convey any part of the estate to the Hospital, nor did they repay to the Hospital the proceeds of sale of the Etherley and Whittle estates. Further, the Corporation did not apply the value of the land in the Close to the benefit of the Hospital but availed itself of its powers (alleged) as the founder of the Hospital and manager of its affairs. Instead of letting the property for benefit of the Hospital, the Corporation occupied the mansion house for successive Mayors of the town, paying only an occupation rent. There is some reason to think that the occupation rent was not paid to the Hospital, but was simply an entry in the Town accounts. In fact, the Corporation never accounted to the Hospital for any of the monies or rents involved and refused to produce any deeds, accounts, papers or writings in its possession, or even show them to the Master, Brethren and Sisters.

The reform of town corporations in 1836 brought the problems of the Hospital and its endowments to a head. The new Newcastle upon Tyne Corporation, by its new name of the Mayor, Aldermen and Burgesses, claimed to be entitled to hold the Mansion House and the Walker Estate as its own property discharged from any trust for the benefit of the Hospital. It also refused to hand over to the Hospital the Mansion House or to pay any rent for it, or to convey any part of the Walker Estate. On 23rd August 1836 the Attorney General and the Master, Brethren and Sisters of the Hospital instituted proceedings against the Corporation in the High Court of

Chancery. The Corporation in effect admitted all the facts but challenged the legal effect and asserted that the Corporation itself was legally entitled to the Estate, free of any trust for the Hospital, and that none of the endowments had ever been properly conveyed to the Hospital and that the Corporation had at all times been in possession. The case came to trial in July 1842, being heard by the Master of the Rolls, whose judgement was that the appropriate proportion of the Walker Estate should be conveyed to the Hospital and that the Corporation should account for the due proportion of income from the Estate, and likewise they should pay a proper rent in respect of the Mansion House. The Corporation then appealed to the House of Lords. Before the appeal was heard the House recommended that the matter should be compromised on terms to be approved by the Attorney General. The terms settled between the Corporation and the Hospital with the approval of the Attorney General were to be incorporated in an Act of Parliament. The Holy Jesus Hospital Act was duly passed (9 & 10 Victoria Cap 39) but this Act failed to include certain alterations and amendments which had been required by the Chancery Court. It was therefore repealed and re-enacted as amended on 23rd July 1847 (10 & 11 Victoria Cap 34).

The effect of this Act was that the Corporation should pay to the Master, Brethren and Sisters of the Hospital £800 annually by four quarterly payments, this sum being charged upon part of the Walker Estate consisting of Byker Hill Farm, Stotts House Farm, Sharpers House Farm, Walker West Farm and Walker East Farm. The conveyances of the Whittle Estate and Etherley Estate to the purchasers were confirmed as also was the Corporation's title to the Walker Estate, including the Lordship of the Manor, freed and discharged from all claims of the Hospital except the annual payment. The Mansion House was vested in the Corporation freed and discharged from all rights and claims of the Hospital, which was increased in size from forty to fifty residents, namely the Master and twelve Brethren and thirty-seven Sisters. The Master and Brethren were to be Freemen without wives who had been resident within the borough for twelve months before their appointments. The thirty-seven Sisters were to be widows or single daughters of Freemen aged fifty or more and they also must have been resident within the borough for twelve months before appointment. The qualification of being poor was defined as not being entitled to any property or income of more than £15 per annum.[3] The Corporation were to appoint the Master and to fill up vacancies and in making appointments they were to give preference to five brethren and five sisters who were entitled to the benefit of the charities of Sir Walter Blackett and Thomas Davison. Inmates of the Hospital were to be provided with four tons of coal per annum, and for the Master and Brethren a coat and to each of the Sisters a gown, thus confirming a long standing practice of the Corporation. The Town Council was empowered to make regulations for the government of the Hospital.

The Hospital's claim upheld by the Master of the Rolls was for the proportion of the Walker Estate which the proceeds of sale of the estates at Whittle and Etherly bore to the purchase cost of the Walker Estate. The Whittle Estate had been sold for £1300 and the Etherly Estate for £1615, making a total of £2,915. The purchase cost of the Walker Estate was £12,220 so that the proportion claimed by the Hospital amounted to 23.8% of the value of the Walker Estate (or the income) and in addition the very substantial sum for rents collected by the Council and not paid over to the Hospital. The income of the Walker Estate was estimated in 1809 to be between £5,000 and £6,000 and a 23.8% share of this could be estimated at around £1,300, and would have been substantially more in 1842. On this basis the finally agreed rent charge of £800 per annum seems very low but it must have been considered adequate and was clearly approved by the Attorney General.

The treatment of the Hospital by the Common Council may seem to be somewhat high handed, but it must be remembered that the Council had itself founded the Hospital, erected its buildings and provided the initial endowments. In addition the scheme to sell the endowment estates at Whittle and Etherly

---

[3] Holy Jesus Hospital Act 10 & 11 Vict. Cap 34 Sec XIX.

using the money towards the purchase of the Walker Estate was intended to benefit the Hospital as well as the revenue of the Town, and the Council was maintaining the Hospital out of the Town's resources. A possible explanation is that the Council discovered very soon after the Hospital was incorporated that a body consisting of thirty-three women and seven men, all of whom were aged, poor and presumably not capable of maintaining themselves, was not really capable of managing its own affairs. The endowments were probably inadequate for the needs of the Hospital but by itself it would have been quite unable to increase its revenue. The estates seem to have produced only £80 per annum and the Hospital's share of the Walker Estate, if the original proposal had been carried out as intended, would have increased the revenue to £185 per annum. The original endowments produced only about £2 for each resident; this would be increased to over £4. This amount was in fact paid up to 1769, and by the late eighteenth century residents were receiving £6 per annum with in addition four wain loads of coal and a coat or gown yearly. About 1809 the money allowance was increased to £12 per annum. Under the settlement established by the Act, this would be increased to about £15 per annum. The value of money at any particular time is notoriously difficult to calculate but for purposes of comparison it may be recalled that the first general old age pension was set in 1905 at five shillings per week, i.e. £13 per annum.

It was unfortunate for the Hospital that instead of obtaining a conveyance of a substantial proportion of the Walker Estate, it was given instead a permanent annual sum of £800. Probably none of the parties involved in the dispute foresaw that the value of the £800 would over a long period of years be eroded by inflation. This did in fact happen and the annual payment became quite inadequate to maintain the Hospital, which had to be supported by funds from the St Mary Magdalene Hospital and partly from the City rates. It was reported to the City Council in 1957 that the St Mary Magdalene contribution to the Holy Jesus had risen from £800 in 1938 to more than £8,000 in 1957. The financial position had become acute in the

1920s. The old Hospital building remained in use until about 1930 when it was considered to be so much out of repair and inconvenient that new arrangements must be made. Accordingly by a scheme of the Charity Commissioners in 1935 a number of small houses were built on the site where they are still in use off Hunters Road. The removal of the Brethren and Sisters from the old building to the Hunters Road houses was completed in 1937.

The St Mary Magdalene and Holy Jesus Hospitals Amalgamated

In 1957 the City Council proposed to amalgamate the St Mary Magdalene and Holy Jesus Hospitals together with three similar but much smaller charities of Thomas Davison, Ann Davison and Sir Walter Blackett. A draft scheme was prepared by the Charity Commissioners and after lengthy negotiations (in which the Freemen were involved) they approved an amended scheme which was duly confirmed by Act of Parliament on 14th May 1959. Under this scheme the incorporated hospitals were dissolved and the Charities placed under the management of the Corporation of Newcastle which was constituted Trustee and was to operate through a committee at least two members of which were to be Freemen nominated by the Stewards Committee.

The provisions of the scheme approved in 1959 were amended in some details by a further scheme of the Charity Commissioners in 1968, under which the Corporation of Newcastle ceased to be the Trustee and a Body of twelve Trustees was set up instead. Four of the Trustees were to be appointed by the Corporation, three by the Stewards Committee and one each by the Bishop of Newcastle, the University of Newcastle and the Newcastle Council of Social Services. These ten were to co-opt two other Trustees to complete the Body of twelve.

These Trustees continue to govern and operate the combined charities in a much wider field than the medieval foundations. The interests of the Freemen of the City have been preserved, whilst the funds of the Charities can be and are applied in various, but largely similar, ways to the benefit of a very much larger section of the general public.

It has already been mentioned that the Chapel of St Thomas the Martyr (known as St Thomas's Church) built in 1830 to replace the Chapel on the Tyne Bridge, had been amalgamated with the St Mary Magdalene Hospital in 1611. This church was separated from the Hospital by the 1968 scheme, becoming a separate ecclesiastical charity under the jurisdiction of the Church of England.

CHAPTER 11

Freemen's Charities

In addition to the hospitals of St Mary Magdalene and Holy Jesus, five other charities are administered by the City Council. Three of these are the hospitals of Thomas Davison, Ann Davison and Sir Walter Blackett. These were in origin small almshouses for poor Freemen and Freemen's widows, set up under the wills of their founders, which are now represented by income from comparatively small endowments applied for the relief of aged Freemen and widows. The beneficiaries of these funds are in some cases also beneficiaries of the larger hospitals but are not necessarily residential and can be relieved separately.

The two remaining charities administered by the City are: a) Thomas Davison Trust Fund. For the assistance by loans to Freemen setting up their own business. Applicants for which must reside in the City and be under 25 years of age; and b) Sir Thomas White Charity. Sir Thomas White, Lord Mayor of London in 1554, who died in 1566, in his will directed that each year the sum of £104 be paid in rotation to certain towns and cities. This fund is available to young Freemen and inhabitants, for one year in a 24-year cycle. £100 was to be loaned in sums of £25 each for 10 years, without interest, no doubt to help them set up in business. The remaining £4 was intended to cover expenses. Newcastle last received the legacy in 1962. Applications for these five charities are made via the Lord Mayor's Office.

The Stewards Committee act as Trustees of two small charities for the benefit of Freemen and their widows and daughters; these are the Harrison legacy, being the income derived from the estate of the late R B Harrison which he bequeathed to the Committee on a charitable trust for this purpose, and the Rebecca Walker Trust, the origin of which is now little known and is therefore worth recording. When the late Mr John Duguid Walker JP (a distinguished Chairman of the Freemen for some thirty years) retired in 1923, the incorporated companies funded a presentation in appreciation of his service. The greater part of the fund was expended in the production of an elaborate volume containing an illuminated address, together with a series of "achievements" of the armorials of each of the existing companies. These were carefully prepared by Miss Elizabeth Davies of Newcastle and signed by all the members of the respective companies. The volume was enclosed in a casket made of oak which formed part of the foundation piles of the Roman bridge over the Tyne at Newcastle, known as Pons Aelius. The casket and volume are at present held on loan by the Newcastle University Library. The funds subscribed exceeded the cost by a small margin and it was suggested that this money should be given to Mr J D Walker's wife Rebecca. She, however, expressed the wish that the money should be invested and the income used at the discretion of the Stewards to provide a consolation prize to a deserving but unsuccessful applicant for a share of the Town Moor money at the Christmas distribution each year. A copy of the Trust instrument forms part of the presentation volume.

The Town Moor Money Charity (already mentioned in connection with the Town Moor) came into existence as a result of the dispute between the Common Council and the Freemen in 1771. The agreed settlement provided, as was later included in the Town Moor Act 1774, that the Stewards could direct up to a total one hundred acres of Town Moor to be leased for seven years for the purpose of cultivation to improve the land. The rents were to be collected by the Town Chamberlains and when they reached a sum of £100 this was to be handed over to a nominee of the Stewards for distribution at the discretion of the Stewards amongst the poor Freemen and widows resident within the town limits. These enclosures came to be known as "intakes". This system still operates with only minor variations but was slightly amended by the Newcastle Improvement Act 1870 and a statutory order of the Charity Commissioners in 1970. Under this order seven Freemen Trustees were appointed to manage the distribution, which has been carefully fitted into the national system of Social Security. Distributions among those entitled under the rules are made in June and December, as has been practised for more than the last hundred and fifty years. The Stewards of the respective companies still assist in the distributions and their knowledge of the individual applicants is invaluable to the Trustees, although much of the administration is managed by the Administrator employed by the Stewards Committee.

APPENDIX 1

Identity of Burgesses and Freemen

The words Burgesses and Freemen are used in a variety of contexts and it is sometimes questioned whether the two words mean the same body of persons. Before and in Norman times a number of towns were styled boroughs, some of the inhabitants being styled Burgesses; in cities they were called citizens, but the same class was meant. The description Borough or Burgh was used to indicate the Town whose Burgesses were entitled to certain privileges (which varied in different towns). The Burgesses were those townsmen entitled either collectively or individually to the benefit of these privileges which depended on or accompanied the holding of a plot of land known as a burgage where the burgess had his house (commonly of wood and often moveable). Such plots of land were held at fixed customary rents and although the Domesday Book did not include the four northern counties, we know from other records that the usual burgage rent in Newcastle was a halfpenny per annum which indicates an early origin, probably pre-Conquest. Many boroughs, created in the Norman period but after the Conquest, had burgage rents of twelve pence. The Domesday Book uses the expression burgess sometimes as meaning the plot of land or its house and sometimes its owner without always distinguishing very clearly between the two ("half burgesses" are mentioned) but it seems clear that the title of the burgess to be a burgess normally depended on his holding land within the borough of which the minimum would be the household plot. He was undoubtedly a freeman, that is to say, free as opposed to being a slave or bound to land as a villein. As a freeman he was entitled and bound to bear arms for the defence of his town and family. The modern burgess or freeman no longer (or very rarely) qualifies by holding a burgage plot or other land within the borough, but instead qualifies by formal admission based on patrimony (hereditary right), service as an apprentice or in some towns marriage to a freeman's daughter.

When written documents, which before the Norman Conquest were rare, became comparatively common in the twelfth century and later the practice whereby the King or one of the greater feudal overlords would grant a written charter to townsmen setting out the confirmation or grant of privileges. We find these charters granted to burgesses, good men, honest men, Freemen and other similar expressions in relation to various towns and the fashion for the word used changed from time to time. Burgesses was probably the most usual but Freemen is used as early as the Domesday Book itself, while Henry II's Assize of Arms 1181 refers to Burgesses and the whole community of Freemen. Most of the Newcastle charters are to Burgesses, but some are to the good men. There is no doubt the same body of persons was intended irrespective of the descriptive word used. King John granted three charters to Newcastle referring or relating to the Fee Farm (rent paid to the Crown). Two of these were to the Burgesses and one to the good men; the latter uses both words[1].

The privileged boroughs became known as free boroughs and this expression was used for legal purposes, e.g., "all the privileges of a free borough". The Burgesses similarly became known as Free Burgesses and those who were entitled to the privileges of a burgess were said to be free of the town (whence we get the expression freedom of the town) and those entitled to this freedom became known as Freemen. The medieval Gilds Merchant set up under Royal Charters not only included Burgesses who held land within the borough, but were also entitled to admit sons and others who were not land owners and later still to admit the apprentices of Burgesses. There thus came into membership persons who were not land owners and they were said to be free of the guild. Membership of the guild conferred freedom to trade in the town and usually also all the privileges and duties of a burgess. The word free in this sense not only refers to free (i.e. non-servile) status but also to the fact that Burgesses' trading operations were often, if not always, entitled to freedom from some local or national financial charges (e.g. Henry II's Charter of 1175 granting freedom

[1] Brand II, p132

from tolls throughout his dominions). Burgesses were described as free of that trade or free of that company when so admitted. No doubt when serfdom died out and free personal status became universal, the free trading sense of the expression became the more important. To this day in some towns the Freemen are officially known as Burgesses and not as Freemen. In many Acts of Parliament including the Town Moor Act 1774, the Newcastle upon Tyne Improvement Act 1870 and the Town Moor Act 1988, the words Burgesses or Freemen are used throughout as synonymous.

APPENDIX II

The Customs of Newcastle upon Tyne

The Customs are contained in a small parchment document (P.R.O. Chancery Misc. Bundle 34 File 1. No 15). It has no date but appears to have been written during the period when David of Scotland was in occupation of Newcastle upon Tyne approximately between 1140 and 1145. For convenience the Customs are shown here as separate paragraphs but this does not appear in the original. Translation from the Latin is as follows:-

These are the laws and customs which the Burgesses of Newcastle upon Tyne had in the time of Henry King of England and ought to have.

The Burgesses can distrain upon foreigners within or without their own market, within or without their own house and within or without their own Borough without leave of the Provost unless the County Court is being held in the Borough, and unless (the foreigners are) on military service or guarding the castle.

A Burgess cannot distrain upon a Burgess without the leave of the Provost.

If a Burgess have lent anything of his to foreigners let the debtor restore it in the Borough if he admits the debt. If he denies it let him justify himself in the Borough.

Pleas which arise in the Borough shall be held and concluded there except pleas of the Crown.

If any Burgess be appealed of any plaint he shall not plead without the Borough unless for a default of (the Borough) Court.

Nor ought he to answer without day and term unless he has fallen into erroneous pleading ("miskenning") except in matters which pertain to the Crown.

If a ship have put in at Tynemouth and wishes to unload, the Burgesses may buy what they will.

If a plea arise between a Burgess and a Merchant it shall be concluded before the third ebb of the tide.

Whatever merchandise a ship has brought by sea must be landed, except salt, and herring ought to be sold in the ship.

If any man have held land in burgage for a year and a day lawfully and without claim, he shall not answer a claimant unless the claimant shall have been without the realm of England or is child not of age to plead.

If a Burgess have a son he shall be included in his father's freedom if he be with his father.

If a villein come to dwell in the Borough and dwell there a year and a day as a Burgess, he shall abide altogether unless notice has first been given by him or by his master that he is dwelling for a term.

If any man appeal a Burgess of anything he cannot do battle with the Burgess but the Burgess shall defend himself by his law unless it be of treason whereof he is bound to defend himself by battle.

Neither can a Burgess do battle against a foreigner unless he shall have first gone out of his burgage.

Any Merchant, unless he be a Burgess, cannot buy of a townsman, either wool or leather or other merchandise, nor within the Borough except from the Burgesses.

If a Burgess incur forfeit he shall give six ounces to the Provost.

In the Borough there is no merchet nor heriot nor blodwit nor stengesdint.

Every Burgess may have his own oven and handmill if he will, saving the right of the King's oven.

If a woman be in forfeit for bread or beer no-one ought to interfere but the Provost. If she forfeit twice she shall be chastised by her forfeit. If three times, let justice be done upon her.

No-one but a Burgess may buy webs to dye nor make nor cut them. A Burgess may give and sell his land and go whither he will freely and quietly unless it be in claim.

The Customs are set out in Latin with translation in a paper by Charles Johnson MA, FSA, published in *Archaelogia Aeliana* 4th Series, Volume 1 (1925). They are also discussed at greater length with background in *The Origins of Newcastle upon Tyne* by R F Walker published at Newcastle in 1976.

APPENDIX III

The Poor Burgesses v. The Rich Burgesses

Exchequer Plea Roll 1305
Public Record Office reference E 13/27 M 60

The following is a translation from the above Plea Roll, which speaks for itself. It is followed by another extract from the Exchequer Plea Roll 1308/9 (reference E 13/32), showing how the suit was finally closed.

"FURTHER OF THE MONTH OF EASTER

Northumberland

The Sheriff of Northumberland made his return before the Barons of this writ under the Great Seal in these words "Edward by the Grace of God etc. to the Sheriff of Northumberland Greeting Whereas our poor burgesses of the town of Newcastle upon Tyne supplicated us by their petition that various injuries and oppressions had been done to them by the rich burgesses of the said town and it was said we would cause justice to be fulfilled and have sent the Petition under our seal to our Treasurer and Barons of the Exchequer charging them that having investigated the said Petition they cause justice to be done to the said poor burgesses in respect of these injuries and oppressions. We charge you that you make known to the said rich burgesses that they must appear before the said Treasurer and Barons in three weeks from the day next after Easter which day we have fixed beforehand for the same burgesses to reply to the poor burgesses in respect of the said injuries and oppression. And have there then this Writ. IN Witness I myself at Westminster the thirteenth day of April in the Thirty third year of our Reign."

On which day the said poor burgesses came and offered themselves against the said rich burgesses and no one replied for them. And because the names of the said

rich burgesses are not named in the Writ it was awarded to
the poor burgesses that they should prosecute their suit by
a Writ to cause the said rich burgesses by name to come to
reply etc. And the Sheriff was directed to cause to appear
in fifteen days after the day of St John the Baptist Nicholas
of Karliol Peter le Grapere Thomas the Clerk Nicholas son
of John Scott John son of Henry Scott Thomas of Karliol
Gilbert Fleming John Torald Walter of Cogeham William
Porter William Heryng John Trotaund Stephen Trotaund
Roger Peytevyn Peter Sweyn John Wodeman John Crawe
Robert of Morpath Gilbert of Fennum William the Tanner
of Tynemouth Thomas of Herteburn William of Oggle
Gilbert of Oggle Robert of Boroudon Adam of Dureme
Adam Bridok William the Draper of Tynemouth Nicholas
of Ellerker John Lobald Thomas of Sylkesworth Thomas
de la Bailly Henry of Neuton John Flemyng Roger of
Hecham William de Burne William of York John of
Reddesdale Adam Fynk Adam Neu of Barnard Castle
Nicholas of Faudon Peter of Housden Adam of Brinkelowe
John Redcale William Russell the Baker Richard del
Howes William of Benwell Gilbert Haukyn Henry Pandy
Adam Elward Thomas Prouor Adam of Galwey to reply to
William le Sadlere William of Dalton Richard of Fennum
Richard of Egermund William Smallegh Walter son of
Richard Thomas son of Richard Adam of Gunter and
other poor burgesses of the town of Newcastle upon Tyne
for various injuries and oppressions done to them by the
said Nicholas and others contrary to the liberties and
customs of the said town etc.

On which day the said Nicholas de Karliol and other
rich burgesses appeared by their attorney and similarly the
said William le Sadlere and other poor burgesses came by
their attorney. And the same poor burgesses pleaded that
whereas by liberty granted by Charters of the progenitors
of the present King Edward formerly Kings of England and
confirmation of the same King they are free and ought to
be free to buy and sell victuals and other merchandise of
whatever kind in the said town of Newcastle and in all

other cities and boroughs in the Kingdom of England just as freely as the said rich burgesses. The same rich burgesses notwithstanding those liberties by a sinister conspiracy between themselves have impeded the aforesaid poor burgesses and up to the present time are still impeding them daily by which they can the less use and enjoy the said liberty. Videlicet if any of the said poor burgesses should make a length of woollen cloth in his house and would wish to sell it by the yard the said rich burgesses in no way allow the said poor burgesses to sell cloth thus by the yard but if they sell the whole in one piece they are heavily fined in the gild of the said rich burgesses. And if a ship loaded with herring comes to the port of Newcastle the rich burgesses do not allow the said poor burgesses to purchase the herring for drying in their own houses just as they themselves are accustomed to do except that which they wish to buy and use in their own homes. And if any of the said poor burgesses buys a tun of wine the rich burgesses do not permit them to sell the tun by the gallon and half gallon or quart in a tavern but if they otherwise sell the whole tun they are heavily fined in the said gild. And they make a common bargain of whatever kind of small goods the poor burgesses buy in the said town. And if the poor burgesses buy fresh skins to be tanned and sold they prevent any doing this; unless the ears of these skins are longer than the horns the poor burgesses are heavily fined in the said gild And that the rich burgesses do not allow the poor burgesses to buy for money or shares wool fells nor wool to be sold by the sack or half sack collected and shipped just as the rich burgesses do, unless they wish to make all the wool into cloth in their own homes for their own clothes and if they do otherwise they are heavily fined in the said gild contrary to the form of the above said liberty. And to the damage of the said poor burgesses One hundred pounds and then etc.

And the said Nicholas de Karliol and others say that the status and condition of the said William le Sadlere and others who have just pleaded as poor burgesses is reduced and ought to be reduced in the matter put forward: the liberty of the said town should be limited in the said matters because they say that the same Nicholas and others have a certain gild merchant in the same town from ancient times formed by the burgesses and merchants of that town which they and their ancestors have had up to the present time And the gild is such that those who are of the said gild can buy and sell freely in the said town without challenge or exercise the same liberties in the said town or in other parts and that other men of the said town who are not of the gild do not have liberties in the same way as fully except as to certain things which the said William le Sadlere and others who have just pleaded have put forward and further that they say that because the same William and others are not of the gild that they ought not to enjoy in this way the liberties which they themselves enjoy and use. The said Nicholas de Karliol and others were questioned if the said William le Sadlere and others who have just pleaded are in the liberty of the said town of Newcastle and if they are tallaged and contributors with other men of the town to all tallages and burdens which fall on the said town? and they do not deny it. What they say and fully concede is that they are in the liberty of the said town and they are tallaged and contribute with the other men of the town to all tallages and burdens which fall on that town. They are again questioned as to whence the said William le Sadlere and others sustain with other burgesses the burdens which attach to the said town? If they have any special privilege by an Act of the King by which those who are of the said gild ought alone to enjoy thus the liberties and others not? Who say that up to now they do not have any special privilege other than that presently used by custom.

And because the said Nicholas de Karliol and others do not put forward any special privilege above the said gild whereby in the liberties granted to the men of the said town by the Lord King they should be separated from others in the community so as to enjoy the said liberties more fully than others who are of the same liberty and bear the burdens of the said town nor have they anything else for themselves other than a custom which is altogether contrary to the laws and justice and to the distinction of the common wealth of the men of the said town it is adjudged that all and singular of those who are of the liberty of the said town and who bear the burdens of the town in the aforesaid form may buy and sell freely individually and in common without any exception just as in accordance with the liberties granted to the men of the said town by the Lord King they can and should do And that they shall do no harm to any of the men who are in the liberty of the said town irrespective of whether they are of the said gild or not nor should any other sue for injuries to the liberties of the said town which ought to be sued for in common.

And that the said Nicholas and other men of the gild shall make compensation in respect of the aforesaid matters in mercy And assessment of the damages of the said poor burgesses shall be placed in the responsibility of the barons who should cause it to be discussed Afterwards the damages are assessed by the Barons at Fifty pounds And the Sheriff is directed to produce this sum from the lands and chattels of the said Nicholas and other rich burgesses who are of the said gild Fifty pounds to those of the said poor burgesses etc.

Damages Fifty pounds whence Ten pounds to the Clerks"

Exchequer Plea Roll 1308/9
Public Record Office E 13/32 Northumberland

"John of Shefeld came before the Barons and produced a certain writing which witnessed that William Sadeler William of Dalton Richard of London Thomas of Leicester Ivo Pistor Thomas Laurence Richard of Fennom Richard of Egremonds William Smalegh Walter son of Richard Thomas son of Richard Adam Gunter and John of Rome the common attorney of the said William and his said associates and other poor burgesses of the town of Newcastle upon Tyne admitted to this by the King's writ acknowledge themselves satisfied by the said John of Shefeld during the time he was Sheriff of Northumberland in respect of Forty Pounds which was due to them out of Fifty Pounds recently awarded to the poor burgesses of the said town of Newcastle before the Barons of the Exchequer against Nicholas de Karliol and other burgesses of the Gild Merchant of the said town by way of damages. And the said John of Shefeld is to render Ten Pounds remaining from the said sum of Fifty Pounds to the clerks of the Exchequer etc. Of which the date is at Newcastle upon Tyne the Seventeenth day of January in the Thirty fifth year of the Reign of Lord Edward the Father of the present King"

(Placita coram Baronibus, 2 Edward II

The Star Chamber Case 1515

The records of this case are printed in full in the Selden Society Volume No 25 (1910) and abstracts are included in a paper on the case by Dr F W Dendy printed in Archaelogia Aeliana Third Series Volume VII (1911). This note is intended to outline the case and to draw attention to some of the essential points.

It is clear from the record that the case arose from the same basic causes as the 1305 Exchequer case, the full Gild meeting in 1342 and similar troubles in 1438, namely maladministration of the Town's affairs and oppression of the lesser Freemen by the greater, including in particular the claim of the lesser Burgesses to freedom of trade. Dendy appears to think that it was a struggle for political power but this seems to attribute ambitions to the lesser Freemen which they may not have intended, though they may well have thought that some additional political power might enable them to correct the oppression and maladministration from which they suffered.

In 1305 it was the poor Burgesses who took action against the rich Burgesses. In 1515 the roles were reversed and it was the rich merchants who took action against the lesser craftsmen alleging that they had conspired together to cause a riot against the Mayor, Aldermen and the merchants. The Mayor, Aldermen and merchants therefore petitioned the King for redress. The lesser Burgesses replied that they were entitled to trade freely in the town but had been unable to obtain justice from the Mayor and Aldermen. It is interesting to note that the Burgesses' answer expressly referred to their rights of free trade and to the ordinances made in 1342, and that they called themselves the artificers, Burgesses and Gild Merchants. It does not appear to have been suggested that the Aldermen and their supporters represented the Gild Merchant.

The King (Henry VIII) and Council appointed commissioners to investigate the matter. They investigated the claims of both parties in considerable depth and examined witnesses at length. Forty-two witnesses gave evidence for the artificers Gild Merchants that they had bought and sold merchandise (not within the scope of the craft company to which they belonged) for long periods without interruption or complaint from the merchant companies. Twenty-nine other witnesses stated that they had bought and sold merchandise but had been required to reach agreement (usually involving a cash payment) with the stewards or wardens of the craft gild which normally dealt with the relevant kind of merchandise. Thirty-nine witnesses, all members of one of the three merchant companies, stated that when buying or selling merchandise beyond that required for the use of themselves or their families the artificers were always interrupted or fined. The Mayor and Aldermen said that time out of mind the custom had been that the craft of drapers was to buy and sell only woollen cloth, the craft of boothmen was only to buy and sell corn and the craft of mercers was trading wholesale and retail all kinds of groceries, merceries and all other merchandise and no other artificer or craft had occupied any of these trades except if it was to the use of his house and household or else was agreed by the merchant companies.

The Court of Star Chamber to which the case was referred was a political and adminstrative court as well as having legal functions and comprised many of the most powerful officials of the kingdom. The case was regarded as extremely important and the hearing was attended on at least one occasion by the King in person. The decision of the court was in effect a masterly compromise between the two parties. It was decreed that members of the craft companies (enumerated at length) could not use the trades of the merchant companies, but which these companies were bound to admit them to membership on payment of specified admittance fees, the amount of which depended upon the financial status of the applicant. These admittance fees virtually excluded the poorest Freemen and made the wealthier pay heavily for the privilege of membership. Thus the monopoly of the merchants was confirmed but the right of the craftsmen to trade was also upheld, subject to their paying for the privilege of admission to the merchant companies.

The court also decreed a change in the method of electing the Mayor and other civic officials, which virtually ensured the power of the ruling class (i.e. the merchants) to control the elections. The Court's decree was confirmed by a charter under the great seal of Henry VIII.

APPENDIX V

Companies of Freemen

The Companies of Freemen active in 1995 are listed below. The dates shown are the most probable date of their Incorporation, however many had been in existence up to a century earlier.

Bakers and Brewers	1342
Barber Surgeons	1442
Bricklayers	1454
Butchers	1621
Colliers	1656
Coopers	1426
Cordwainers	1566
Curriers	1546
Goldsmiths	1536
Hostmen	1600
House Carpenters	1579
Joiners and Cabinet Makers	1589
Masons	1581
Master Mariners	1536
Merchants	1216
Millers	1578
Plumbers and Glaziers	1536
Ropemakers	1648
Saddlers	1459
Sailmakers	1663
Scriveners	1675
Shipwrights	1636
Skinners and Glovers	1437
Slaters and Tilers	1451
Smiths	1436
Tanners	1532
Taylors	1536
Upholsterers	1675
Weavers	1527

The Armorial Bearings
of the Incorporated Companies
# of Freemen

BAKERS & BREWERS

BARBER-SURGEONS & CHANDLERS
(now known as Barber Surgeons)

BRICKLAYERS & PLASTERERS
(now known as Bricklayers)

BUTCHERS

COOPERS

CORDWAINERS

**FELT MAKERS, CURRIERS & ARMOURERS
(now known as Curriers)**

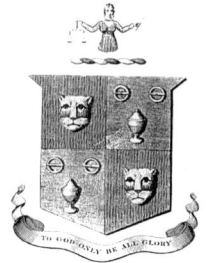

GOLDSMITHS

HOSTMEN

HOUSE CARPENTERS

JOINERS

MASONS

MASTERS & MARINERS

MERCHANT ADVENTURERS

MILLERS

PAVIOURS **(previously Colliers, Paviours & Carriage men, now known as Colliers)**

PLUMBERS, PEWTERERS & GLAZIERS
(now known as Plumbers)

ROPERS
(now referred to as Ropemakers)

SADDLERS

SCRIVENERS

SHIPWRIGHTS

SKINNERS & GLOVERS

117

SLATERS
(now Slaters & Tylers)

SMITHS

TAILORS
(now styled as Taylors)

TANNERS

UPHOLSTERERS, TIN PLATE
WORKERS & STATIONERS
(now known as Upholsterers)

WEAVERS

Armorial Bearings taken from: The Armorial Bearings of the several Incorporated Companies
of Newcastle upon Tyne by James Walker & M. A. Richardson, published in 1824.

APPENDIX VI

Newcastle upon Tyne Town Moor Act 1988

Section 18

SCHEDULE
Enactments Repealed

Chapter (1)	Short title (2)	Extent of repeal (3)
14 Geo. 3. c. cv.	An Act for confirming to the resident Freemen or Burgesses, and resident Widows of deceased Freemen or Burgesses of the Town of Newcastle upon Tyne, their full Right and Benefit to the Herbage of the Town Moor, Castle Leazes, and Nun's Moor, within the Liberties of the said Town, for two Milch Cows each, in such manner as has been used; and for improving the Herbage of the said Town Moor, Castle Leazes, and Nun's Moor, respectively.	The whole Act.
7 Will. 4 & 1 Vict. c. lxxii (1837).	An Act for regulating and improving the Borough of Newcastle upon Tyne.	Sections 123 and 155.
28 & 29 Vict. c. ccl.	Newcastle-upon-Tyne Improvement Act 1865.	Sections 12, 13 and 14.
33 & 34 Vict. c. cxx.	Newcastle-upon-Tyne Improvement Act 1870.	Sections 6 to 22, 24, 25, 29, Schedule 2, Schedule 3 and Schedule 4.
45 & 46 Vict. c. clxxii.	Newcastle-upon-Tyne Improvement Act 1882.	Sections 14, 52, 53, 57, 77 and Schedule 2.
55 & 56 Vict. c. ccxxxvi.	Newcastle-upon-Tyne Improvement Act 1892.	Sections 104, 105, 106, 108 and 120.
61 & 62 Vict. c.ccxxvii.	Newcastle-upon-Tyne Corporation (New Infirmary Site) Act 1898.	Sections 2 to 4 and 6 to 8.
62 & 63 Vict. c. cclxv.	Newcastle-upon-Tyne Tramways and Improvement Act 1899.	Section 33.
4 Edw. 7. c. ccxx.	Newcastle-upon-Tyne Corporation Act 1904.	Section 105 and 106.

Chapter (1)	Short title (2)	Extent of repeal (3)
1 & 2 Geo. 5. c. lvi.	Newcastle-upon-Tyne Corporation Act 1911.	Sections 43 to 48.
7 & 8 Geo. 5. c. lvi.	Royal Victoria Infirmary Newcastle-upon-Tyne Act 1917.	Sections 2, 3 and 4.
16 & 17 Geo. 5. c. cii.	Newcastle-upon-Tyne Corporation Act 1926.	Section 35 and the Schedule.
25 & 26 Geo. 5. c. cxxiv.	Newcastle-upon-Tyne Corporation (General Powers) Act 1935.	Section 115 and Schedule 3.
15 & 16 Geo. 6. & 1 Eliz. 2 c. xl.	Newcastle upon Tyne Corporation Act 1952.	Section 58.
2 & 3 Eliz. 2. c. xxv.	Newcastle upon Tyne Corporation Act 1954.	Sections 2 and 3.
4 & 5 Eliz. 2. c. lxxxi.	Newcastle upon Tyne Corporation Act 1956.	Sections 4, 5 and 6.
8 & 9 Eliz. 2. c. xli.	Newcastle upon Tyne Corporation Act 1960.	Sections 4, 5 and 6.
1964 c. xxxv.	Newcastle upon Tyne Corporation Act 1964.	Sections 4, 5, 6 and 7.
1980 c. xliii.	Tyne and Wear Act 1980.	Part I of Schedule 5.

BIBLIOGRAPHY

I Books Relating to Newcastle

BOURNE, Rev. H.	History of Newcastle (Newcastle 1736)
BOYLE (and KNOWLES)	Vestiges of old Newcastle (Newcastle & London 1890)
BRAND, Rev. J.	History of Newcastle (London 1789 2 vols)
BROWN, J.	Short Account of the Freemen (Newcastle 1823)
CHARLETON, R. J.	History of Newcastle (London 1892)
CLARK, J.	Freemans Pocket Companion (Newcastle 1817)
COLLIER, J.	Essay on Charters (Newcastle 1777)
DENDY, F. W.	Three Lectures on Newcastle (Lit & Phil Soc 1921)
FRASER, C. M.	Life and Death of John Denton AA[4] vol 37 (Newcastle 1989) Mediaeval Trading Restrictions AA[4] vol 39 (Newcastle 1961)
GARDINER, R.	England Grievance Discovered (London & Newcastle 1655, 1796)
GIBSON, J. F.	Historical Sketch of Newcastle (Newcastle 1888)
GRAY, W.	Chorographia Survey of Newcastle (London 1649)
HOWELL	Newcastle & the Puritan Revolution (Oxford 1967)
HEARNSHAW, F. J.	Newcastle (London 1924)
JOHNSON, C.	The Customs of Newcastle AA[4] vol 1 (Newcastle 1925)
NEWCASTLE JOURNAL	Report of Parliamentary Commission Enquiry 1833 (published by Newcastle Journal, January 1834)

I Books Relating to Newcastle (cont.)

OLIVER, A. M.	Early Newcastle Deeds (Surtees Soc vol 137 1924, Durham & London)
RICHARDSON, M. A.	Newcastle Reprints (7 vols Newcastle 1849)
COMMITTEE OF STEWARDS	Petition etc as to New Roads (Thompson Newcastle 1771)
WELFORD, R.	Newcastle & Gateshead 3 vols (London 1887)
WALKER & RICHARDSON	Armorial Bearings of the Companies (Newcastle 1824)
WALKER, R. F.	The Origins of Newcastle (Newcastle 1976)

II Books of General Relevance

BALLARD, A.	Borough Charters (Cambribge 1913)
GROSS, C.	The Gild Merchant (2 vols) (Oxford 1890, 1964)
MAITLAND, F. W.	Township and Borough (Cambridge 1898)
MEREWEATHER & STEPHENS	History of the Boroughs of the U. K. (London 1835)
STUBBS, W.	Select Charters 8th ed. (Oxford 1895)
SYKES/FORDYCE	Local records (3 vols) (Newcastle 1867)
SELDEN SOCIETY	vols 18, 21, 25, (London 1903-1910)
SURTEES SOCIETY	vols 50, 93, 101, 105, 117, 137.
TAIT, J.	The Mediaeval English Borough (Manchester 1936)